"This book is not only ⟨...⟩ Muslim young woman ⟨...⟩ Jesus—but also an insightful story ⟨...⟩ point of view. Rose Masih shares her struggles and joys to help people see what Islamic life can look like, and to testify to the saving power of God through Jesus Christ. It is an eye-opening book and highly recommended!"

—David I. Yoon, Ph.D.
Lead Pastor, Good News Church
Instructor of Biblical Studies, Emmanuel Bible College
Research Fellow, McMaster Divinity College

"Rose Masih has a delightful way with her pen, telling the very personal, and sometimes painful story of her walk out of a deeply Muslim community toward Jesus. She opens her heart to tell of her hunger for the Bible and her longing to know the God of the Bible and His Son, Jesus. She tells of companions and miracles along the way that can only be explained as the loving hand of God providing and protecting her along this precarious journey. Hers is a story of courage and sacrifice, as well as a story of the goodness of God and His great love. Get a cup of coffee...you are going to enjoy this book."

—Mark L. Maxwell
President, Prairie College

"Part memoir, part window into a culture that is largely hidden from view in the Western world, *From the Curse to the Cross* is a fascinating story that proves that when one seeks the truth, one finds it.

It is a must-read for anyone who seeks to better understand what life can be like for men and women living in Muslim countries and the joy that comes from faith in Jesus, despite its dangers. It is an inspiration to live more brightly for Christ."

—Rev. Dr. Marc Potvin
Pastoral Leaders Development Associate, Canadian Baptists of Ontario and Québec

"This gripping story is beautifully and simply told. It reveals the incredible love of Jesus, who patiently pursues even those who initially shake their fists at him. Like the merchant in Jesus's parable of the Pearl of Great Price, Rose Masih traded everything she had in exchange for a relationship with the living Lord Jesus. May all who read her compelling story discover the One who captivated Rose's heart is worth it all."

—Dr. Susan Booth
Professor of Evangelism and Missions, Canadian Baptist Theological Seminary and College

"*From the Curse to the Cross* is both a personal testimony and theological reflection upon what it means to follow Christ after growing up as a Muslim. Rose Masih opens up her life with great courage and the Bible with fine precision. Not simply a theological treatise, Rose explores how The Holy Spirit has actually worked in her life as seen through the lens of God's Word. Want to know how to best reach the new Muslim neighbours in your city? Looking for a way to help Muslim-background believers belong to your Christian community? Or just want to be inspired by God's work in one woman's life in ways that are both probably quite exotic and strangely familiar? Then *From the Curse to the Cross* is for you."

—Rev. Jacob Birch
Director of Philanthropic Partnerships, Canadian Bible Society

"*From the Curse to the Cross* is a riveting real-life story of God's rescue from darkness and despair to a life of freedom and promise. Rose Masih opens her life to us as she invites us to join her on this journey. You will be so captivated that you will not be able to put this book down. I recommend this book to those who may feel imprisoned and wondering if there is a way through. God will make a way as He did for Rose, revelations and miracles, and then her willingness to obey and trust. May you find Hope as you read."

—Major Everett Barrow
Officer/Pastor, Salvation Army

"*From the Curse to the Cross* is one woman's triumphal journey from darkness to light, from her confusion in fundamentalist Islam to freedom and purpose in Jesus Christ. As in the book of Esther, the true hero on every page of this story is not so much Rose, Esther, nor Mordecai, but the Holy Spirit working in and through them to change the world for the glory of God. You will both weep and cheer as Rose bravely shares her story of God's call on her life."

—Pastor Todd Harris

"Many Christians in the Western world pay very little price for following Jesus. While we live in a post-Christian culture, it is still one that tolerates Christianity. Rose Masih shakes us out of our comfort as she shares her story of growing up in the Middle East and becoming a Christian. She does not hide her own prejudices against Christians before her conversion but invites the reader to walk with her on her eventful journey."

—Dr. Stephen J. Bedard
Pastor, Brookfield Baptist Church

"I have heard of stories of God doing miracles in the lives of Muslims, drawing them to himself. Now I have read the story of my friend Rose Masih who has had that experience. What surprised me, however, was not just the powerful way that God worked and is still working in Rose's life, but how God used her story to challenge my own faith as a follower of Jesus. Do you have 2 hours? Read the story of how God transformed the life of this Muslim woman if you dare. You will be transformed also."

—**Cam Roxburgh**
Global Director, Forge Missional Training Network

"A life's story can both highlight God's grace and a person's perseverance. Reading this story has been a great encouragement to me. It points to God's gracious love in our world."

—**James Watson**
Instructor, Tyndale University

"This is a powerful story of a girl that grew up in the Muslim faith, from a young age to her teens and beyond. The story tells of how she began to question the Muslim faith and how the Lord called her to Him. You will read about the trials and tribulations this girl went through and how she has been blessed by the Lord."

—**Laurel Steeves**
Financial Administrator, Baptist General Conference of Canada

"Rose Masih's book is a compelling account of her journey to finding Jesus. Masih writes with such simplicity and profundity that readers will find it challenging to put the book down. There were times when I couldn't help but wonder whether I would have such trust and faith as Masih did when confronted with life-altering crossroad moments. Anyone who is looking for an honest, daring, and courageous story about the cost of following Jesus and bearing witness to God's providential care, this book is for you."

—**Justin Napier**
Sessional Instructor for Chaplaincy and Spiritual Care, Booth University College

"Rose Masih and her husband have been my friends for several years. I have attended the international church they have planted.

I was privileged to read an early manuscript of Rose's dramatic (and traumatic) story and journey to faith. Her life and her story have been a huge blessing and encouragement to me as I see that the power of God to save and transform lives is not limited to the book of Acts. It has continued throughout history right up to the present day. I pray God will use Rose's story to impact the lives of many – to encourage believers and to save unbelievers."

—Pastor Rob
Retired pastor and missionary

"When Rose Masih first shared her story with me, I was amazed at her courage and fortitude. This book is a young woman's story of rising above misogyny and hate to find freedom in Christ. This story of Rose's journey is a must-read for anyone struggling to leave a life of oppression."

—Rev. Dr. Keith Daly
Retired pastor, Christian Baptist Church Newmarket, ON

"Rose Masih, my former student, provides a beautiful narration of her journey from Muslim orthodoxy to acceptance of Jesus as Son of God, Savior, and Lord. Her conversion to Jesus came at a price since she had to flee her family and home country to exile in Canada. Rose's biography makes fascinating reading."

—Dr. James A. Beverley
Research Professor, Tyndale University

To Kevin,

FROM THE CURSE TO THE CROSS

Rose

FROM THE
CURSE TO THE
CROSS

HOW JESUS
SAVED A MUSLIM
WOMAN FROM
THE CURSE

ROSE MASIH,
M.DIV.

Printed in Canada

ISBN: 978-1-4866-2235-1
eBook ISBN: 978-1-4866-2236-8

Word Alive Press
119 De Baets Street Winnipeg, MB R2J 3R9
www.wordalivepress.ca

WORD ALIVE
—P R E S S—

MIX
Paper from
responsible sources
FSC
www.fsc.org   FSC® C103567

Cataloguing in Publication information can be obtained from Library and Ar-
chives Canada.

DEDICATION

This book is dedicated to my Lord and Saviour, Jesus Christ, who broke my chains, gave me freedom, released me from the curse, and brought me from darkness into light.

I also want to dedicate this book to my wonderful and loving husband. Without his continued support, it would have been impossible.

I would also like to thank my beautiful children who supported me in every possible way while I was working on this book. They have been my greatest source of encouragement and joy.

CONTENTS

ACKNOWLEDGEMENTS

I would like to acknowledge my friends and colleagues in ministry who supported me in various ways. Thank you, Dr. Susan Booth, Professor of Evangelism and Mission, Canadian Baptist Theological Seminary and College, Cochrane, Alberta; Dr. Keith Daly, Retired Senior Pastor Christian Baptist Church, Newmarket, Ontario; my professors Dr. Wafik Wahba, Dr. Kevin Livingston, Dr. Dennis Ngien, Dr. Arthur Boer and Dr. James Beverly from Tyndale Seminary, Toronto, Ontario; my congregation, as well as my dear friends Curt Fletemier, and my "sister" Vanessa Venafro. Without your support and constant guidance, it would be impossible for me to be where I am today.

Bible colleges and universities that played a major role in forming my spiritual life:

Booth University- Winnipeg, MB
RZIM Academy- Atlanta, GA
McMaster Divinity College- Hamilton, ON
Tyndale University College and Seminary- Toronto, ON
Prairie Bible Institute- Three Hill, AB
Uganda Christian University- Mukono, Uganda
Pakistan Bible Correspondence School- Pakistan

English translations of the Arabic and Hindi words used are in footnotes throughout the book.

PREFACE

W hy did I write this book?

After two decades of living as a Christian, I feel that God wants me to share my life with the world. He has done great things for me. This isn't my story—it is His story of saving me, not only from the curse I was under while living away from him but from eternal damnation.

"Jesus answered, 'I am the way and the truth and the life. No one comes to the Father except through me'" (John 14:6).

Who is this book for?

This book is for everyone, for Muslims, Christians, and atheists. It is for those who have no faith, those seeking God, and those who are struggling with faith.

My journey to Christ contains phases where I experienced each of these phases. I started as a Muslim; I experienced Christianity, and then I was lost for a while. I was seeking God, but I didn't know it. When things got tough, I struggled with my faith. I experienced pain, suffering, and almost denied God or any god.

In the end, the true God triumphed and gave me life. I desire to share this journey with you, my readers, and hope you will experience the same life.

INTRODUCTORY REMARKS

As a Muslim, I never thought that one day I wouldn't be a Muslim. I believed in Islam wholeheartedly. I adored Mohammed and took pride in knowing that I followed the only true and purest form of religion on the face of the earth. I did everything that a devout Muslim should do.

I read the Quran daily, reciting and memorizing important passages. I prayed five times a day called Namaz.[1] I fasted in the month of Ramadan and paid my zakat alms on time. I fed the poor whenever I could. I gave expensive offerings to the saints' temples called Mazars.[2] I attended Islamic teachings called Majlises[3] seminars and took pride in leading religious processions for Mohammed and Allah. There isn't a single thing that I didn't do to please Allah and secure my place in heaven. I desperately wanted my good deeds to outweigh my bad deeds on the day of Qayamah[4] (Judgment Day), so I would be allowed into paradise.

In my school years, I even persecuted and oppressed Christian and Hindu students in the name of Jihad (striving for one's faith,

---

[1] Muslim prayer ritual five times a day.
[2] Mazars: the graves of Muslim saints adorned by flowers and rose flower sheets. Famous Mazars are the main attractions in the city. People from all over the country come to particular temples to pray to the dead saint for healing or restoration of relationships, etc.
[3] Majlis: Islamic teaching seminars or symposiums.
[4] Qyamah: Judgment day in Islam.

and in my case, it was Islam). I remember a Hindu girl named Vidya, a quiet, little girl in my classroom. I was probably in grade two or three. One day I spat in her lunch and told her to eat it because I was told the night before in my Islamic class that Hindus drink cow's urine.

After that incident, I enjoyed teasing her every day whenever I had a chance. I was cruel and heartless, thinking I was doing Allah a service. After a while, she stopped attending, and now I think it was because of how I treated her and made fun of her religion. I was proud of myself, following in the footsteps of my beloved prophet. I was proud, thinking that, even though I was young, I could help the cause of Islam.

I looked down on non-Muslims and hated Jews with a passion. I thought my mission in life was to destroy Jews and convert Christians. I was taught that Hindus are worse than Christians as they don't share a holy book. So I looked at them as animals. I was a proud Muslim, Sunni girl for the first eighteen years of my life.

Learning about Christians and Jews was part of our Islamic school, but I was taught the distorted version of Christianity and Judaism. I was taught that Christians and Jews lost their Holy books long ago. They had manipulated and corrupted Allah's sacred texts: Torah (the Pentateuch), Zaboor[5] (the Psalms) and Injeel[6] (the Gospel). I was taught that Allah hated them because they changed his holy books. I was also taught that one day all non-Muslims would become slaves of Muslims. In my birth country, non-Muslims are given a derogatory title as Bhangees[7] (sweepers)

---

[5] Zaboor: Muslims believe that God sent four books, including the Quran, to his favourite prophets. Zaboor was revealed to David.
[6] Injil: the Gospel. Muslims believe that the Gospel was revealed to Jesus Christ (Isa in the Quran).
[7] Bhangee: a derogatory term often used by Muslims for non-Muslims. They clean toilets and manholes. Muslims believe that only Christians and Hindus should do janitorial work.

and are mostly given jobs as toilet cleaners. I was told that the land of Israel belonged to Palestinians. Jews were evil, and the West and the Americans helped them take land away from Palestinian Muslims. Israel will never be at peace because this land belongs to Muslims, and Allah will give victory to Palestinian Muslims one day. They have special favour from Allah. All Muslims must unite to free Palestine from the evil hands of Jews. I was passionate about this cause and attended many protests and conferences to support Palestine, chanting "Death to Israel."

I believed with my whole heart that Christians (even though they are considered 'people of the book'—Ahl-e-Kitab[8]) still commit the gravest of all sins—Shirk. I was taught that this is the only sin that Allah (even if he wanted to) can't forgive. Shirk is an Islamic word, which means sharing Allah with someone else. Christians say that Allah had a wife and a son, and for that, Allah hates them. I was zealous for Allah and his messenger—Rasool-ullah[9] Mohammed. I was willing to do anything I could to save, defend, and spread Islam.

Among my brothers and sister, I was the only one with this much devotion. Sometimes when I talked about Islam and how I was willing to give up my life, my mother would get scared. My religion was everything. I was proud that I belonged to the best religion.

I didn't know that in merely a few years, my world would be turned upside down.

---

[8] Ahl-e-Kitab: "the people of the book." Christians and Jews are called "people of the book" because, according to Islamic tradition, Allah sent three books before he sent the Quran.

[9] Rasool-Ullah: "Messenger of Allah", a common title for Mohammed.

THE FORMATIVE YEARS

None of my siblings had my zeal. I was the second oldest of four sisters and four brothers. My older sister married an older man when she was young, and we didn't spend much time together, so I have few memories of us playing together. As far as I remember, I was always the oldest.

I finished reading the Quran in Arabic (which is not my mother tongue) at seven. By ten, I had memorized half of the Quran. I arranged praise songs for Mohammed called Naat Khawani,[10] and Quran readings and recitations in Arabic called Quran Khawani[11] at my home every month.

Our Quranic teacher was an elderly lady we called Ustani Ji,[12] which means "woman teacher." She taught the Quran to the girls on our streets for free as her service to Allah. She believed that in exchange for every girl who read the Quran in Arabic, Allah would reward her with a place in paradise called Jannat.[13] She was kind, gentle, and used to give us treats for our accomplishments.

She was also a good storyteller. She told us good stories about Mohammed. My favourite was about Mohammed and the Meccan

---

[10] Naat Khawani: praise songs for Mohammed. This is an event highly respected, especially among Sunni Muslims.

[11] Quran Khawani: a recitation of the Quran. This is a highly respected act of worship performed by Muslims every day, especially during holy days and months like Ramadan. Muslims believe that reading and reciting the whole Quran pleases Allah very much.

[12] Ustani Ji: a respected woman teacher. Muslims in Asian cultures never address their elders, especially their teachers, by their names. They always give them respected titles.

[13] Jannat or Jannah: a view of paradise in Islam.

woman who threw garbage at him every day. One day, when she didn't throw garbage at him, Mohammed became concerned and visited her house and saw her lying on her bed. He asked her why she hadn't thrown garbage, and she responded that she was sick. Mohammed took care of her, and because of his compassion, she became a Muslim.

After hearing this story and seeing how Mohammed treated this woman with respect and dignity, he became my hero. I was surrounded by vicious and abusive men, including my brother-in-law. So, hearing these stories about Mohammed made me happy.

But as we graduated from lower grades to higher grades in our Quran classes, our teacher started telling us another story to inspire us to make the right choices as growing girls and women. It was a story about Mohammed visiting heaven and hell. The story goes something like this:

One day Mohammed was visiting heaven and hell. When he was doing a tour of heaven, he saw beautiful heavenly young women who were created solely for pleasuring faithful Islamic men, but he couldn't find a single earthly woman. He was puzzled and asked Allah, "ya, Allah, where are all the women I know on the earth? Where are they?" Allah and his angels told him, "You will see them soon."

When his tour of heaven ended, they took him to the place called hell. There was smoke and fire everywhere. As Mohammed walked, he saw many women he knew hanging with hooks in their breasts, and some of them were hanging with their hair on top of a burning pot or fire. Many had poisonous lizards stuck on their eyebrows, biting them. These were the women who shaped their eyebrows. Some of them had snakes and scorpion-like animals on their lips and over their bodies. There was a demon standing at every woman's head holding a whip made of snakes, whipping them, and snakes would bite them with every strike. These were the women who wore makeup, didn't listen to their husbands, and didn't cover their faces or wear burqas.[14] So, Allah hated them and sent them to hell to live forever.

As a six- or seven-year-old child, I heard this story, and I was scared for months. I didn't want to go to hell, and I did everything to please Allah. I challenged myself to follow Allah all my life, and even if I had to sacrifice my life for him, I would do it so I could get to heaven and not hell.

I became even more zealous, seeking any way to please him. It was this motivation that made me hate Christians and Jews. I took every opportunity to tell Christians about Allah. We had no Jews in my birth country at that time, so I never directly interacted with them.

I'm not going to lie—hating was easy and sometimes enjoyable. Every time I made a Christian or Hindu cry, I felt proud of myself. I wanted to please Allah and Mohammed. I proudly called myself 'Ashiq-e-Rasool,'[15] which means "lover of Mohammed." Everything I did was out of love for Mohammed.

I never thought that in a few years, my world would be shaken, and everything that I held dear about Islam and Mohammed would no longer make sense. I never imagined that a day would come when, instead of burning with hatred for Christians, I would be consumed by the love of Jesus Christ and would be willing to give up my life to follow Him.

Today, I can say with pride in my voice that after spending almost twenty-four years with my Saviour and my Lord, Jesus

[14] Burga: a garment covering made of loose black fabric worn mainly by Middle Eastern and Indian Muslim women. A hijab is just the head-covering part of it. According to Arab and Islamic traditions, Muslim women should cover themselves in these long flowing garments.
[15] Ashiq-e-rasool: a title used by Muslims to show their devotion to Mohammed. It means "lovers of the messenger Mohammed." Even though Mohammed's name is not added in the title, it is only used for Mohammed.

Christ, my love for Him is growing every day. My passion for reaching out to the lost and proclaiming the gospel has only increased. Jesus has proved Himself to me as the *only one* and *true God*. Again and again, He has shown me His unconditional love. He doesn't keep count of my past sins and has forgiven me completely. I can say with confidence that I don't have to be scared of hell—He took my hell upon Himself on that cross. I know I'm forgiven. Not because of what I do, but because of what He did on the cross for me.

Today I want to invite those Muslims who are reading and don't know the Jesus Christ of the Bible to come to Him. He loves you despite your hatred. He is ready to forgive you. He has eternal life. You don't have to work hard to earn points in heaven. There will be no scale in heaven to weigh your good and bad deeds. Jesus Christ is the ultimate scale. Put your trust in Him. Confess your sins to Him, and in return, "He will prepare a place for you in heaven."

My Prayer:

This is my sincere prayer for everyone reading my story. May the God of the Bible speak to you and lead you to His Son Jesus Christ, who alone is "the way, the truth and the life." He is the "gate to heaven."

I also pray that you will find the truth you are seeking in Jesus Christ, and this truth will set you free. I pray that you will be free from the fear of hell and that you will know that you are being justified before God because of His Son Jesus Christ.

Amen

CHAPTER 1

WOMAN—"YOU ARE ONLY HALF A MAN"

The loud sound of drums from our street watcher woke us at 4:00 a.m. He was playing loud drums and announcing on his loudspeaker—"*Jagtay Raho*[16]—Wake up sleepers, it's *Sehir*[17] (breakfast) time. Ramadan Mubarak."

I loved Ramadan, but Sehri wasn't my favourite time. I've always been a sound sleeper and love my sleep. Morning prayers (Namaz) were also not my favourite, but the fear of hell usually woke me up on time. My mother used to tell me that I could sleep even in the middle of bombs exploding all around me. I love sleeping.

I remember that year Ramadan came in December. I was happy about this because I didn't like the summer heat. It was cooler than usual in December, or maybe that was how I felt in the wee hours of the morning, after waking up and ceremonially washing my hands and feet for 'wudu'[18] before I read my Quran or prayed my prayers.

After eating a large buffet breakfast, which was usually cooked by our live-in Bengali cook, Mustafa, I convinced my sister to go for a walk in the cool of the morning before the Mulla[19] (Muslim

---

[16] Jagatay Raho: means "Wake up" or "Keep waking up."
[17] Sheri: a word used for waking up before sunrise to prepare breakfast in the month of Ramadan.
[18] Wudu is a term used for ceremonial washing before prayers and touching the Quran.
[19] Mulla: an Islamic cleric.

cleric) would call for Azan, the call to prayer on loudspeakers. My sisters and I wore our sweaters, covered ourselves with thick cashmere shawls, and headed to the main door.

The aroma of Parathas,[20] omelettes, fried vermicelli, toasted bread, and homemade yogurt drink was in the air. Most homes on the streets had their lights on. From the cracks of the windows of some houses, we could see the flashing lights of colour or black-and-white television sets. As my sisters and I were walking out the door, I heard a set of footsteps running behind us. As I turned around, Mustafa (whom my father adopted when he was just a boy) approached us. Although he was a lot older, he called me "Sister," and he called my father "Big Daddy." "Baji[21] (sister), Baray Daddy[22] has told me to accompany you. It isn't good for women to go alone outside."

I was sixteen and had become a little rebellious, so I didn't like his comment. I said, "I'm not a child. We are going to be fine. You can go wash dishes or something."

"But Baji," he responded, "Baray Daddy told me you are only half a man, and I'm not to leave you." Baray Daddy's command was more important than the opinion of a sixteen-year-old girl who was only half a man. I also didn't like that statement.

I never understood why girls always had to be watched. Why couldn't they play cricket in the streets like their brothers or go out for a short walk? Why couldn't my sisters and I go outside in our safe and posh neighbourhood? Why did this dirty servant always have to watch us? He smelled like eggs, fish, and sweat (but I didn't say that to him). I shrugged my shoulders and said, "Whatever."

My mood was ruined. We didn't enjoy our walk with Mustafa following close behind. I never suggested to my sisters that we go

---

[20] Parathas are Indian flat flakey bread, a breakfast staple
[21] older sister
[22] Big daddy

for a walk or do anything that involved going outside after that day, especially when my father was present. I always prayed for him to be on some mission trip.

But that cold December Sehri morning during Ramadan, I learnt something—women would never have the same freedom as men. We would always be second-class citizens like prisoners in our own homes. My father would always trust his male servants more than his daughters. We would always be 'half of a man.' I didn't like this revelation.

A NOTE ABOUT FASTING AND RAMADAN:

Fasting in the month of Ramadan is one of the five sacred pillars of Islam. In retrospect, fasting in Islam now seems very strange. Muslims wake up before sunrise to prepare their breakfast. They usually prepare a big breakfast, three or four dishes and eat as much as possible until the sun rises. Then they don't eat or drink until sunset. They break their fast again with a grand meal at sunset, eating as much as they can. They repeat this cycle of special meals at sunrise and sunset for Ramadan. So, basically, Muslim people skip lunch and call it a fast.

Muslims all over the world celebrate Ramadan in the same month. I have recently seen a rise of Ramadan signs and posters in grocery stores and public squares in North America. I've met several Christians and non-Muslims inspired by the Islamic fast. They praise their Muslim friends and acquaintances for their strength and courage about sacrificing their meals to feel the pain of hunger and starvation.

In reality, I think anyone can skip lunch and go without eating or drinking for the day with a kingly meal in the morning and another for dinner. I haven't had a proper lunch in my life for over thirty years. I sometimes don't drink anything during the daytime. Does this mean I've been fasting for thirty years?

CHAPTER 2

A Big Day!

It was a big day for me. My dad and I were going to pick up my progress report card for class eight. I had studied hard, and I wanted to prove to my father that I was smart.

I wanted to continue my studies. My older sister married when she was very young and now had a terrible life. I saw her pain and suffering, and I didn't want that for myself. I didn't want my father to marry me off to a much older man, which he had already mentioned would happen to those who didn't study well.

When I turned fourteen, I was told that he was committing a great sin by not marrying me off. I wanted to go to college or university, and possibly even leave the country to attain higher studies. But I would be allowed to continue only if I met my father's standards.

I silently recited all the verses I remembered from the Quran. I truly wanted to make him proud. All my life, I wanted to please men to gain their approval. First, Allah and Mohammed, and then my father.

"Please, God, help me this time." I prayed. "I want to be a good daughter."

Before we stopped at my secondary school, we stopped at the elementary school to pick up the report cards for my two younger brothers. They had both failed, and their teachers had many complaints about their behaviour.

My father was distraught, which scared me. He had spent a lot of money on our school tuition by sending us to one of the best schools in the city.

I could hear my heartbeat—in fact, it almost felt like my blood had stopped flowing. Every gland of my body released sweat. Every step felt heavy as we marched towards my classroom.

I don't know how we made it to my classroom, but soon there I was, standing in front of my teacher, Miss Rehana.[23] She had her long, silky, black hair down and had worn extra lipstick. She looked pretty.

I loved Miss Rehana.

"Hello, Mr. Shah," she said as she came towards us, "thanks for coming today," welcoming my father with her magical smile.

"Waleikum assalam (peace be unto you)," my dad responded with the common Islamic greeting.

To me, she seemed a little embarrassed. I got the impression that she already disliked him, and I wasn't sure what she would say next.

She told me to stand outside and asked my father to go into the room with her.

Once they had disappeared into the classroom, I ached to know what they were talking about. I strained hard to hear them but couldn't make anything out.

"Come on in." Miss Rehana said a few minutes later, calling me into the classroom. She had a smile on her face as she pointed at the empty chair beside my dad.

"Here, sit down."

I looked at him from the corners of my eyes.

He was sipping a cold bottle of Coca-Cola—the drink which he often said was made by Kafirs.[24]

---

[23] Not her real name.
[24] Kafirs: infidels.

He looked relaxed and even wore a smile. He was staring at my progress report in disbelief.

As I approached to sit next to him, he stood from his chair and hugged me.

"Shabash Baita,"[25]he began. "You have raised my head today. I am so happy. You are my lion. You are allowed to choose your courses for class nine, and if you continue like this, I will send you to college also."

I couldn't believe my ears. I looked at Miss Rehana and saw her wide smile.

It turned out that I had topped not only my class but my entire school.

I later learned that Miss Rehana had convinced my father to let me continue, and I will be forever grateful to her. She told my father that my English was extraordinary as she was also my English Grammar teacher. She had never seen someone speak English as well as me.

I was happy that I would be allowed to continue my education. In fact, that was probably the happiest memory of my childhood.

I said to myself after that event, "After all, my father might not be that bad."

After we left the school, my father lectured me on how privileged I was to continue. He lectured that he was trusting me and told me in a threatening way the consequences of breaking that trust.

On the way home, we stopped at the store because he wanted to buy my favourite ice cream. My report card had been so good that it made him forget my brother's bad report cards.

When we came home, I expected him to beat or punish my brothers, but to my surprise, they weren't punished at all. I

---

[25] The word *shabash* means good job or well done. *Baita* means son but is used often for daughter as well.

thought maybe I made him so happy that he didn't want to ruin this moment.

But I was wrong. My brothers didn't get punished because they were men. Males in my family had a privileged position, and they could get away with anything.

The following year my younger sister didn't do well. She was beaten with sticks and threatened to be given in marriage to a much older man. My dad told her that girls were already a burden, bringing shame to their families when they fail at school. It was a matter of status for him. With girls, his reputation was at stake.

It was different for boys. Even though my brothers failed year after year, they would be the ones to carry on his name, so there was no strict punishment for them.

I was afraid of upsetting my father. I wanted him to be happy with me so I could go to college. Even in the summer vacations—that is what they are called in my country—equivalent to summer break here, I was bringing books from the library to read. Cell phones, the Internet, and computers weren't a thing back then. I discovered my love for books and made them my best friend at a young age. I remember saving money to buy books that I loved. I loved reading fiction, action, thriller, sci-fi, and alien worlds. I wasn't allowed to read romantic novels because those were considered inappropriate and would have poisoned my mind.

We had a pretty good library in our school, but I read almost everything interesting they had in that library. One day, I heard about this new library close to my school. It was a huge building and had thousands of books on every topic in the world (that's what I thought).

I asked my father to get me a membership for that library. His immediate response was no. I couldn't understand why he was so against it, but later I found out that the library was owned by some European organization I don't remember now. But I was persistent, and without his knowledge, I got the library membership. As I recall, that was the first thing I did against my father's wish. It was the beginning of my rebellion.

CHAPTER 3

MY "ILLICIT" ACTIVITIES

"Girls, I don't expect any silly behaviour from you. Your father isn't home, so you must behave," Ammi[26] (mother) announced.

"Where is he this time?" I asked.

"He went for Hajj (pilgrimage), and then he is going to Qatar for some Tableegh (Dawah),"[27] Ammi responded.

"Great, so we can watch TV past nine!" I exclaimed.

"Yes, but only on weekends," Ammi said.

I remember some of the happiest days of my childhood were when my father wasn't in the country, and I knew he was far away, unable to come home charging at us.

On that particular day, Ammi looked tired, so she went to bed early. I wanted to do something fun. This was my opportunity to do something I would never be able to do again. I'd heard about this new arcade place at the corner of our street, next to the little library that I loved.

I clearly remembered Ustani's story about women in hell, but I still wanted to go to that new and exciting place. I wanted to be

[26] *Ammi* means mother in the Hindi/Urdu language
[27] Tableegh or Dawah: a term used widely to tell others that this person or group is engaged in spreading Islam or inviting the world to accept Islam. "Dawah" is the word used in North America and the West. In Islamic nations, it is called "Tableegh."

like a boy. Something took over me during those years—perhaps a spirit of rebelliousness! I knew girls weren't welcome there, but I wanted to go so badly. I'd made friends with a bold girl in school who lived a few blocks away. She was like a tomboy. That day we decided to try Dubbo,[28] the games they had in that place. She was older, and for some reason, the boys at the Dubbo place respected or maybe feared her. That day, we went to play Dubbo.

I loved the energy and the game of Carim[29] board and Packman gaming machines in the arcade behind us. Now and then, I would get panic attacks while in Dubbo thinking about my father. Even though he was thousands of miles away, the thought was constantly haunting me—'what if he sees me here?' I knew if he saw me there, he would immediately kill me. But despite being fearful, I wanted to be there. Something inside me wanted to stay and take risks. And I thought so far everything looked fine. Who was going to tell him? No one knew where I was that day.

Mustafa, our dad's spy, had no idea about my activities, so I thought everything was fine. I was becoming confident and complacent in breaking the rules and climbing boundaries, but that was my mistake.

One day, that sneaky, smelly chef of ours caught me red-handed and threatened me. "As soon as Baray (daddy) arrives from Dubai, I am telling him what kind of girl you are." I knew Mustafa well by then. He was supporting his family in Bangladesh. He had a sister, Chanda,[30] that he wanted to marry off with a big dowry.

So, I made a deal with him. "Okay, you can tell Baray (daddy) that I play Dubbo in his absence. The worst that will happen to

---

[28] *Dubbo* refers to a place where young people gather together to play board games, etc.
[29] *Carim* is a big board game
[30] Not her real name

me is he will beat me. But if you keep this secret, I will give you all my pocket money which will help your family and specially Chanda." He loved his sister dearly.

At first, Mustafa claimed that he'd never take a bribe from a woman for her "illicit activities" (that's what he called it), but later he agreed. He actually became our 'partner in crime' as we needed someone in Dubbo to support us. This was the beginning of my little rebellious life.

I graduated from class ten with flying colours, and (as my father promised) I went to the dream college I always wanted to attend and studied alongside boys. I chose commerce and accounting over medicine because I wanted to become a successful businesswoman, just like my dad. I was happy with my life, especially about changing my dad's mindset about girls being a burden. I didn't know what was waiting for me at college.

CHAPTER 4

New Year—New Promises

"It's a new year, and I'm going to be a good Muslim woman. I will be like my father and spread Islam and convert many people to Islam. It is the only true religion. I wish I could go see Amna Baji every day." As I was getting ready to attend the Muslim sisters' group, I was thinking these thoughts.

As I became more rebellious outside religion, I became more religious in my religion classes. I wanted to know why women were treated differently, so I joined a group of Muslim women who gathered every week to read and recite the Quran and discuss women's issues.

Ever since I joined this group, I felt empowered as a woman. "Today we are going to sing praises to my beloved Prophet Mohammed PBUH. What an awesome day it will be," I smiled.

As I was putting on my hijab with my jeans and long shirt, my mother stormed into my room and asked, "Where are you going this early in the morning?"

"Oh, I forgot to tell you, Amna baji[31] has invited me for Naat khuwani (singing praise songs for Mohammed) in a women's meeting today. We will be setting up loudspeakers on some houses. You know most of the houses belong to Kafirs (Christians). We will surely make them jealous and may invite them to become Muslims," I answered with a big smile and a twinkle in my eyes.

---

[31] Not her real name

"Do whatever you want. No one listens to me anyway," she answered and stormed out of my room. *"What's wrong with her? I am trying to be a good Muslim girl here,"* I thought to myself and shrugged, *"Whatever."*

"I am particularly very happy about today because I learned a whole "naat"[32] in Arabic, the most beautiful language of all and the heavenly language of Allah. Amna Baji will be very happy with me," I thought.

My mother never liked Majlis[33] (Islamic gatherings) or sending us to mosques, but she was disciplined about praying five times a day and keeping all the rituals of Islam. I learned the Quran from my mother's friend at her home and finished it at the age of six years. By nine years old, I had memorized half of the Quran in the Arabic language. And now I had learned a whole praise song to Mohammed in Arabic.

My mother was never a talker. She only said a few things, and if we didn't respond, she never repeated it. I found her always tired and distant, always taking care of my younger siblings. I didn't have a good relationship with her or my father. I was close to my little sister, but I never had parents who supported me in fulfilling my dreams or desires. I guess it was a typical way of raising children in my culture. Parents always seemed distant and unreachable. We were only instructed to listen to them, obey them, respect them—even if they were wrong—and do whatever they wanted us to do. We never questioned their decisions and blindly followed what they said.

Now I was doing things that weren't approved by my mother and some bold things that definitely weren't approved by my father, like playing out in the Dubbo place alongside boys.

---

[32] *Naat* is a praise Song for Mohammed
[33] Majlis: large gatherings similar to conferences and seminars where a guest speaker or expert on a special topic is invited to give a speech.

I was trying to figure out my place, and that was why I joined this group of my Muslim sisters, and I thought my mother would appreciate it, but she clearly didn't.

But I went to these meetings anyway. When I arrived at the meeting point, we all were bussed to different locations. I knew where my group was going, and the whole way, we were talking about how we would be so blessed singing these songs and praising our beloved prophet Mohammed.

As we set up loudspeakers right on top of the Kafirs' (Christians) houses, I thought, *"Now when I sing this Naat in Arabic, I am sure Allah will shake them up and convert their hearts, and they will become Muslims. But if they remain Kafirs after listening to this beautiful song, may Allah's curse be upon them and burn them in hell."* I shared my thoughts with Amna Baji.

"Well done, sister. You will definitely make Islam proud. These Kafirs don't deserve to live," cheered Amna Baji, and all the sisters in my bus proudly pat me on my shoulders. My confidence level was shooting above the roof. I thought I had found a purpose and meaning for my life that day.

When my time came to sing, I closed my eyes, and with complete devotion, I started singing "Lam yat-e-nazir."[34] My voice was heard in the streets, coming from those powerful loudspeakers. I sang the whole song without looking at the paper. I was so proud, but I didn't feel great when I finished singing.

"I don't know what's wrong with me," I thought after I was done. I was hoping for some supernatural incident, but nothing happened.

I was frustrated because I didn't know what I was singing. It was in Arabic, and no one could tell me what I just sang. I came home feeling empty and exhausted, and my throat was hurting. It

---

[34] Words of the praise song in Arabic

15

was hot and humid. Amna Baji didn't bring water with her, and no Kafirs came out of their homes recanting Christianity to fall at our feet and ask how they could become Muslim. No one got shaken up, and no one stepped up and accepted Islam. I felt defeated. I went into my room, closed the door, threw my body on my bed, and started crying. I didn't know why I was crying, but I cried for hours.

"It's Isha[35] prayer time. Wake up." My father had sent my younger sister to tell me. I had already missed Mughrib[36] prayer. I didn't want to wake up to pray, but I had no choice. The only time I was allowed to skip the prayers was when I was menstruating, and my mother used to keep a record of my dates. So, I went for prayer and asked forgiveness from Allah for missing my earlier prayers and performed all the things I was supposed to do.

It was the first time I remembered feeling empty during my prayers. It was also the first time I thought about the words I used for prayers. None of the words made sense to me because they were all in Arabic. Every prayer has the same verses that Muslims are supposed to recite. The only difference is how long they are repeated and said.

That day I was thinking, *"What did I just pray? What did these words, verses and poems mean?"* After that, every time I sat on my prayer mat to pray, it became a routine. I started asking questions in my heart because I was too afraid to raise them out loud.

After that day, I attended many Majlises[37] with Amna Baji, but I wasn't on fire like I was before. In fact, I started asking questions after almost every Majlis from Amna Baji—questions about Mohammed and his many wives, especially the child bride, Aisha.

---

[35] Last prayer of the day
[36] Second last prayer of the day at sunset
[37] Islamic Gatherings

Amna Baji never had answers for me. I felt Amna Baji and many sisters started hating me for asking those questions. One day, Amna Baji told me in front of the room filled with women who used to praise me for my passion and boldness for Islam that I was definitely going to hell because I had doubts about the way we do things in Islam, about our beloved prophet Mohammed, and my role as a Muslim woman. I remember that day I cried so hard the whole night. When I woke up in the morning, my head was hurting so bad.

I didn't know what was happening to me. I was losing interest in my prayers and my reading and recitation of the Quran. I believed Amna Baji that I might be possessed by some unclean spirit and end up in hell. I remembered Ustani Ji's story when we were little about women in hell. I didn't want to go to hell, but I didn't know what to do with my brain, which was constantly raising those questions. I was hurt, alone, and in deep stress, and I had no one to talk to.

CHAPTER 5

HAWA—EVE

"Assalamualaikum[38] (peace be unto you), my name is Hawa. What is your name?" As I looked up, I recognized her. She was the same girl sitting next to me that day when Karim uncle (our driver) had arrived late.

"Walaikumsalam, (peace be unto you, too) my name is Rose," I responded. "Do you want to go to the canteen with me? I am hungry," I asked her right away.

"Sure," Hawa[39] replied.

This was the beginning of our friendship. We hung out every day for hours from then on.

"I really love Hawa. She is my good friend. It is amazing how comfortable I feel when I am with her. She makes me happy. And she is also just like me. She listens to my concerns, doubts, and fears about Islam and Prophet Mohammed without hating me or cursing me. I feel so secure when I am with her," I often thought.

I didn't know that in my zeal for Islam to make Allah and Mohammed happy, I was challenging the true God. When I set up those loudspeakers on Kafirs' homes on Mohammed's birthday, I thought that Christians would be challenged and may even reject Christianity. But I was really challenging the one and only true

---

[38] *Assalamualaikum* is an Islamic greeting
[39] Eve

God—their God. And their true God responded to me by sending Hawa into my life, His true child.

Over the next few months, Hawa became my best friend. I felt like I could share anything with her. Whenever I saw her, I would shout with excitement "Oh, thank God you are here. I was looking for you." And every time we talked, I had something to tell her about my father or brother-in-law.

"You know my father sent my sister back to her abusive, alcoholic husband again." Hawa knew all about my dislike for the men in my household.

One day, I visited my older sister, and while I was sleeping in her living room, I felt someone's presence. I woke up and turned on the flashlight I had with me. It was my brother-in-law, completely drunk, standing at my headrest, staring at me. He got scared of the light and left the room. I told my sister the next morning, and she defended her husband, which upset me. I decided I would never visit her again, and I never did. I was hurt that she didn't believe me.

When I shared this with Hawa, she told me to forgive my sister. I didn't know how to process that. Hawa was my friend, and instead of talking bad about my sister, she encouraged me to forgive. My problems and hatred for men so consumed me that I didn't pay much attention.

Another day, I saw Hawa and asked her, "Why doesn't anyone answer my questions about Allah and Mohammed?"

I knew she also had no answers, but I was frustrated with the world, with men, and with my life.

I often told Hawa that I felt as if everyone in my family and Islamic school hated me because of the questions I raised. I wanted my brain to stop working, but I couldn't help myself. Sometimes I felt like killing myself so this pain would end.

In those moments, Hawa always encouraged me and showed me the bright side of life.

The day a man in my family tried to grope me, I came to college crying to my friend, "Hawa, today I feel so disgusting being a woman. Why do we have to suffer in silence? Why do we have no rights and freedom?"

Hawa cried with me that day.

Another day, I had an argument with my mother. She told me that they would marry me off as soon as I finished college.

I didn't want to get married. I wanted to study and become something. My mother said firmly that girls weren't supposed to study this much, but I did, so I better not abuse it.

I was tired of being reminded that I was a woman and had to live for someone else.

During those days, I saw my older sister a lot. She tried to talk to me, but I didn't want to talk to her because of what had happened earlier. But that day, when she came home, she looked different.

I heard her crying and begging my father not to send her back to her abusive husband, but he sent her anyway. I knew something was wrong, but I didn't dare talk to my father. I came to my college with a heavy heart and talked to Hawa.

We sat under that big neem tree and sobbed for hours about how we felt in our womanhood.

CHAPTER 6

THE DAY THAT CHANGED EVERYTHING!

It was one of those days when I needed to get out of my home and go to college so that I could talk to Hawa. The weekend was horrible. My sister came home with a broken arm. Her husband beat her because she fought with him over his new bride. He brought her home from his supposed police training camp. It turned out he never went for training. He and his mother went to their tribal area in their province, and he had a big second wedding there. He had the audacity to even take his son of a few months with him, leaving my sister and their first-born girl at home.

All his relatives participated in his second wedding ceremony, and no one bothered to tell my sister. My sister thought he was on his police training and missed her son and husband. She wasn't just hurt emotionally. She was beaten by him, his new wife, and his mother because she didn't let his second wife into the house. She was thrown out of her house with her daughter and was told to accept the new wife or go to her father's house.

She chose to seek her father for help, and when she asked him to help her, he responded coldly, "You should be proud of your husband and help him. He is only following Sunnah (Mohammed's teachings). He married that poor girl, his first cousin, to help and support her after her father's death. What kind of a Muslim woman are you? I didn't raise you to dishonour the traditions of Islam and disrespect the Sunnah of our Prophet. Listen to me very clearly. I am not going to keep you here. You must go back to him and do as he says."

I felt like someone had pierced my heart. I was hurt seeing my sister go through this horrible ordeal and my father's response to her. I was scared, confused, and angry. I was angry at my father, the male-dominated society, Allah, and especially at Mohammed. Why did he have to set such an example? When I arrived at college, I told Hawa everything. I don't remember now, but I even said some terrible words about Mohammed, too, I think. Hawa responded, "I'll pray for you, and I will ask my father to pray for you too."

"I don't know what you mean. I pray five times a day (Namaz)," I responded.

"Oh, I thought you knew. I am a Christian, and in our religion, we pray for people who are in trouble," she kindly explained to me.

As soon as I heard she was a Christian I screamed, "WHAAT, are you Kafir? You never told me that! How dare you? I have been eating with you, sharing my life with you! How can you do this to me? You made me unclean. I have become unclean. Before I do something stupid, get lost, I don't want to see your face again!"

I was crying and screaming at the same time to which she quietly responded, "I am so sorry. I thought you knew about my religion, but if you ever want to talk to me again, you will find me in that church." She quietly pointed to the big cathedral that I had seen since I was a child but had never stepped inside, across the street from my high school building.

"Hmmm, as if I will ever need help from a Kafir. Allah forgive me," I smirked.

That day I was hurt and broken. I had no idea what I would do with my life. I felt like I had lost everything and had nothing left to live for. Life had no purpose or meaning. I wanted to die. I wanted all the girls to die. I wanted to ask Allah why he allowed this. But there was no comfort, no answer, nothing—just a very long silence.

CHAPTER 7

THE MOST PAINFUL AND HEAVY STEPS

"I told you, you cannot stay here. You have to go back." My father was scolding in a harsh voice. I peeked into the living room. It was my older sister again. Her husband continued to mistreat her. He slept with his second wife in their old bedroom every alternate day, and when he did, she slept outside. She was bawling her eyes out, but my father had no mercy in his voice.

My younger siblings and I (six of us) weren't allowed in the living room when we had visitors or the door was closed. It meant something important was happening, but lately, I was becoming curious about everything, so I eavesdropped because I wanted to know.

"Daddy, I want a divorce. I don't want to go back. He is an alcoholic. He beats me all the time. No one loves me there," my sister explained.

"It is final. I told you. He is only following Sunnah by marrying his poor cousin. She needs support. It is your fault that he beats you. You should have listened to your husband. You will never live here. That (your husband's house) is your home. You will only leave there when you die. I am calling Karim (our driver). He will drop you off at your home," my dad responded coldly.

I felt sudden hatred for my father, men, Islam, and Mohammed.

"What if Daddy marries me off to someone like this man? No, I will never let this happen. I will die before I marry anyone," I thought.

I didn't know when or how I reached college. That day I wanted my friend Hawa. I searched for her everywhere, but she was nowhere to be found. And then I remembered, she told me, "If you ever want to talk to me, you will find me in that church...."

"Oh, it's Sunday today. A lot of people are going into the church. Let's see if she's there," I said to myself.

I started walking towards the church. It felt like every step I took had fifty thousand pounds of weight on it. My heart was racing. Every gland in my body was sweating. I could hear my heartbeat.

Those few steps were the most painful and heavy steps I've ever taken.

Most wealthy Muslim families in my country take pride in sending their children to Catholic Convent Schools. They are considered the best schools in the city. They brag about sending their children to English Medium school where most of the staff is British, or fathers and nuns give instructions only in English. In fact, most of these families try to talk to their children in English at home. At the same time, they hate America and Western nations. They ridicule, persecute, and oppress churches and Christians. I didn't understand this double standard until I became a Christian myself. So, I went to a convent school built under colonization almost two hundred years ago. It was a huge property owned by the Roman Catholic Church in the middle of the city. The property had a few Elementary and Secondary schools, a housing complex for fathers and nuns, a beautiful huge cathedral, and several colleges. It was like a small city within a city.

My college was located directly across from the church. My elementary school was adjacent to the church building, but we weren't allowed to set foot in the church. So I never stepped inside the church compound, but that day, everything changed for me— forever.

CHAPTER 8

THE CHURCH OR HEAVEN?

"Beta (daughter), can I do something for you?" the priest asked me.

"Where am I? Oh no, where is everyone?" I asked.

"The service is long over. You've been sitting here for the last thirty minutes crying," the priest explained. "Can I do something for you?"

"No, no, it's not true. I just walked in," I said to myself and ran out of the church building.

I don't know what happened. I remembered that when I went inside, there were voices singing something in a different language. The tall cathedral ceiling made me feel tiny. The sunlight through the stained-glass windows looked magical. There was a huge cross on which the statue of Jesus was hanging. I couldn't bear to walk anymore. I froze in the place where I was. I felt my body collapse on the bench closest to the main door. I didn't understand anything, but I felt a presence that I had never felt before.

I started crying. I didn't know why, but I remembered crying, actually sobbing. I felt like I was the only person there other than that life-like statue of Jesus Christ. He was far away on the wall, but He felt so close. I felt like I could reach Him and touch Him. I felt His warm embrace, a feeling that I had never felt before.

I didn't remember seeing people. All I remember was walking to the front, taking something from an angel's hand and putting it in my mouth.

I felt in my heart that this was where I belonged. I felt like I was home. I felt like I had found what I had been seeking all these years.

My hurt, anger, pain, all resentment and bitterness, was gone. I just needed to sit there a little bit longer. Maybe I would sit there for the rest of my life.

That was when I heard this voice "Beta (daughter), can I do something for you?" the priest asked me.

"Where am I? Oh no, where is everyone?" I asked.

He disturbed my dream and brought me back to the real world.

When I realized I was in the church, I ran outside as quickly as I could without answering him.

I thought, *"What was this place; did I go to heaven?"*

But then it dawned on me. "Ya, Allah, my mother was right. They have bewitched me."

My mother always warned me to be aware of Christians because they did witchcraft in the church. One step in the church would turn me into a witch.

I was very scared, but I was also very happy.

I cried out, "Ya, Allah, what did I do? Please forgive me." I was confused.

I wanted to hate this experience. I wanted to justify that I just went in to find Hawa, and I fell into the trap of witchcraft. But these things didn't make sense. I knew I was making these things up. I wanted to go back inside and live there for the rest of my life. At the same time, I wanted to leave there as fast as I could.

"What if Karim uncle saw me coming out of the church? What if someone tells Daddy? He would kill me." I trembled with fear.

I came home that day and took a long bath reciting Quranic prayers. I remember cleansing myself from this great sin, sitting on my prayer rug, opening my Quran, and trying to read it.

After reading a few verses, I lost interest in reading the Quran. The scene of heaven I had experienced in the church came before my eyes. I was sitting on my prayer rug with the Quran in my hands, and the church scene was in my heart. I wanted to go back to the church and ask someone about what had happened to me. Even if it was magic, I wanted to get it. I just wanted to be in the church. I realized that day that I had no hatred left in my heart for Christians. Actually, I wanted to know more about them. I wanted to just sit at the feet of the statue of Jesus that I saw in the church. I wanted to live for Him, and I didn't even know what that meant at that time.

CHAPTER 9

THE SPIRITUAL STRUGGLE

"Okay, don't worry. Tomorrow you can talk to Hawa about this (the church experience)," I assured myself and slept. That night for the first time in a long time, I slept peacefully and woke up refreshed the next morning. Everything looked new that morning. I had this feeling like someone who is in love. I didn't even know why I felt so refreshed and happy.

When I went to college the next day, I went to our regular meeting place under the big old neem tree in front of the library. I waited for Hawa there for almost an hour, but she didn't come. I checked in the library. She wasn't there either.

I waited for her under that big old neem tree every day, but she didn't come. I asked my other friends if they had seen her somewhere or knew about her. They told me that they didn't know anyone by that name. They were mad because, for a few months, I had been sitting separately from them. They made fun of me, saying that I had an imaginary friend.

"Maybe they are just playing with me," I told myself. "Maybe they are fooling around."

"Let me ask the registrar," I thought. But they had no information about a girl named Hawa.

"No one knows about Hawa. How can it be? Maybe she left. Maybe she is scared after my last backlash. Maybe she left the college,"

I thought. I was devastated. It was months, and Hawa was nowhere to be found. I even visited the slum near my college where she said she was from, but it was a huge area, and finding a girl there was like finding a needle in a haystack.

I had no one to talk to about what happened in that church. I didn't want to believe what I felt in that church was real. I didn't want to like it. I wanted to hate it so badly, but I couldn't. Another Sunday was fast approaching, and my mind was playing games with me. I was going insane. I was scared as I completely lost interest in reading or reciting the Quran or Namaz (my Islamic prayers). Ammi and Daddy had no idea about my struggle, about my apostasy. I was scared, confused, and worried.

Another Sunday came, and I had no choice but to go to my college. The open doors of the church were calling me, inviting me in. I tried to resist my urge to attend, but I couldn't. I wanted to go in so badly. I wanted to be with these people that I didn't even know. I wanted to hear that heavenly sound of the singing. I wanted to smell the old wood in the church ceiling. I wanted to sit on the last wooden bench. I wanted to be there. I wanted to feel at home. So, I went to the church again. I thought, *"Maybe today I will find Hawa there."*

But I didn't find Hawa. Once there, I didn't even think about her. I was enjoying the scene. The Catholic father (priest) in his white robe and the voices of angels singing and echoing through the rooftops. These people I didn't know somehow felt like a family to me. They sat in the pews with their heads down, listening to the choir singing and the priest talking.

There was a pin drop silence when the priest called them for prayers. Kneeling, men, women and children, old and young families sitting together, were silently saying their prayers. There were no separate quarters for men, women, and children. Everyone was praying together, sitting side by side. "What is this place? Who are these people? What makes them look so peaceful?"

I felt a sudden rush of love for these people who I used to hate and was even willing to kill. I felt tears rolling down my cheeks. I heard myself confessing my sins to myself. I remembered how wrongfully I had accused Hawa and pushed her away. I remembered all the wrongs I did to these people and many others. I was a proud brat raised in a home where value is based on a person's status and race or ethnicity. Something taught me that day that whatever I had learned from my childhood was all wrong. It wasn't from God. There wasn't anything pure or holy about it.

I cried and cried until I had no tears left. I was sitting on that last wooden pew for hours thinking about their Jesus, staring at His statue at the front. I didn't know what to do next, but I knew that day that this Jesus was different than the Jesus I knew from Quran, and that day I decided I wanted to know Him.

When I came home and sat on my prayer mat, I thought about the Jesus I met in the church. I couldn't perform my Islamic prayers after that day. I sometimes just sat on my mat pretending to be praying, but actually, I was thinking about church, Jesus, Christians and Christianity. I didn't know anything about Christianity. All I knew from my experience in the church was that these people weren't evil. I didn't find witchcraft or child sacrifice practises in the church. I didn't see men and women doing indecent actions. Yes, they were sitting together with their families, but there was something beautiful about this mixed gathering.

That day I had a revelation. What if my Islamic teachers had lied to me about Christianity? This idea wasn't pleasing. It was hurtful, and I felt like someone had kicked me in the stomach. I had this deep feeling that there was more to Christianity than I had been taught or told.

Even after developing strong feelings about Christianity, I sometimes had doubts. I found myself struggling and often battling the thought that *"only Islam is the true religion. Only Allah is the true God. Christians are the greatest sinners of all. They are mushraqeens[40] (worshippers of three gods). They have committed the mother of all sins—Shirk.[41] They think Allah has a son, and to prove this, they have changed the Bible. The Bible they have is corrupted. They believe Allah has a wife."* I sometimes wanted to convince myself that I would never follow this false religion called Christianity, but I knew I was lying to myself. I knew I was saying these things because I didn't want to acknowledge my love for Christianity and Jesus Christ.

I remembered how peaceful I felt in the church. I remembered all the times I heard messages from Amna Baji and my Islamic studies teachers about Hazrat Isa.[42]

I was taught that Isa (Jesus) was the only prophet born without an earthly father. He was the only prophet who could heal people and raise the dead. I was torn between two worlds, but something or someone was telling me to seek more, to find out more about the Jesus of Christianity, but who would tell me? I was scared to ask anyone. If I asked my Islamic teachers, they might be suspicious of my interest in Hazrat Isa. If they found out that I went to the church, I would be severely punished. Should I approach the priest in the church? But I was scared. I had no one to talk to. I felt so alone.

I sometimes cried for hours. Part of me hated thinking positively about Jesus, loving Christianity, and doubting Islam. I cried and asked Allah to show me something or do something to

[40] *Mushraqeens* are people who share or associate deities with God.
[41] *Shirk* is the sin committed by mushraqeens, that God has a son and a wife. Sharing God with other non-god beings.
[42] Islamic name of Jesus Christ

stop these thoughts. I begged him for hours to give me peace, but there was no comfort, no peace, nothing from Allah. As always, a very long and painful silence.

I didn't know what to do. I was going into a deep depression. I had no one to talk to. I was alone. I didn't want to go to college anymore because I was afraid that I would end up in the church again. If someone saw me there, they would report it to my father, and he would beat me or kill me. As a girl in that country, I had very few rights. It would have been labelled as an honour killing, and my father would be hailed as an Islamic hero.

Maybe if I worked somewhere, that would take my mind off Christianity. Women were only allowed to work as schoolteachers. It was considered a noble profession in my culture. To this day, teachers are given the right to discipline the children in whatever way they feel right. My father respected all my teachers. I knew it wouldn't be difficult for me to ask him to allow me to teach in an all-girls school, but I was wrong.

When I asked him, he got upset and told me no woman from his family was allowed to work outside the house. But I was very stubborn. I kept pushing him, and after a long fight and hunger strike, my father finally allowed me to work in a school. I was the first woman in my family to work outside the house. It was the start of many firsts as a woman in my family. So, I started teaching as an English language teacher.

CHAPTER 10

THE ESCAPE

I loved teaching, and it became my escape from my spiritual battle. My school became my place of refuge. It was a modern English Medium school. Most of my colleagues weren't interested in praying five times a day. They usually talked about their kitty parties and new places in town that they explored. Some of them were divorced, re-married, and some were single parents. They were all proud Muslims, but they weren't interested in Islam. This was a perfect place for me to work. I didn't have to pretend to pray in front of them. I didn't have to pretend to be a practising Muslim as none of them were, and they usually looked down on people who were traditional or practising Muslims like Miss Aisha.

One summer break, Miss Aisha visited her brother in New York City. She showed us jeans, beautiful sleeveless T-shirts, and sarees she bought to wear while in NYC. She was planning on having a full blast in NYC. She cut her hair in a short bob just before the summer break. She proudly showed off her five-year multiple entry visit visa to all the staff. We pretended to be happy for her, but most of us were extremely jealous. After all, she was going to visit the great nation of the USA, the land where dreams come true. And then we went on our summer break.

Summer breaks were particularly hard for me as I had to be at home for June and July. It was difficult for me to pretend to be a

Muslim anymore. When I taught in school, I only performed one nightly prayer just before my bedtime. On the weekends, I usually had college work to do. But I had no escape during summer breaks. I was stuck at home, and I had to perform my prayers, but I slowly continued to lose all interest in Islam. I wanted to go back to the church, but I didn't know how.

After the summer break, we went back to school. I saw a lady in a hijab and loose clothes sitting in the staff room. As soon as I entered, she ran towards me and hugged me. I was almost an hour early on the first day of school. To my surprise, it was Miss Aisha. I was totally surprised at her transformation. She was a very modern and liberal woman before she left for America. She returned as a devout, fanatic Muslim covered in a hijab from top to bottom.

She told us all her adventures about visiting her brother in the USA. She proudly proclaimed how she learned truly to be a Muslim in the USA. She told us she was so surprised to see her brother and his family committed to the local mosque and their Quranic teachings. They prayed five times a day regularly, fasted in the month of Ramadan, and attended their mosques without making excuses. She mentioned how her nieces and nephews proudly covered their heads with a hijab even though they were born and raised in the USA. For weeks, she was going on and on about how awesome her experience was to be a Muslim in the USA and how she learned to be a true Muslim while she was there. She also decided to leave her daughter in the USA under the care of her brother, so she could also become a good Muslim like her American cousins.

After seeing Miss Aisha's transformation from a liberal woman to a devout Muslim, especially her testimony of how Islam was spreading fast even in America, I became even more confused. I thought something was wrong with me. Perhaps I had some spell cast on me or maybe a demonic possession. If Islam wasn't the true religion, it wouldn't have spread in the USA. Maybe I had hoped that Miss Aisha would return from the USA as even more modern or liberal or even as a Christian. I wasn't expecting her to visit a Christian nation and return as a pious and devout Muslim.

So, I started visiting Muslim saints' temples to find answers. The more I saw, the more confused I got. One temple was the temple of a famous saint. Thousands of devout Muslims visited this temple from all over the country to get their prayers answered.

I visited that temple almost twice a week and sometimes more as it was close to the school where I taught. I prayed to the saint to take away my desire to go to church and for help to become a good Muslim. I offered money and sacrificed animals. I gave alms to the poor, but nothing happened. I had no peace in my heart. If anything, I was becoming more restless.

I didn't realize that I was now openly defending Christians. I had no idea why I was doing it. I was getting irritated at home when I was asked to read the Quran, pray, or fast in the month of Ramadan. My mother started praying over me. She thought I had some jinn (demonic) possession. I cried bitterly at night when I was alone. I wanted to go to church, but I didn't know how. I had nowhere to go, no one to talk to. I couldn't tell anyone what was going on inside me. I was lost, ashamed, and scared. Every day I woke up feeling guilty about my secret sin of liking Christians and loving Christianity. I wasn't in physical pain, but the internal pain I felt was excruciating. I didn't understand why I couldn't go back to the life I had before I stepped into the church. I was sad, angry, alone, and hurt. Little did I know that God was working behind the scenes and preparing a way for me.

CHAPTER 11

THE JOB OFFER

It was a day for a parent-teacher meeting. A child in my class had ADHD. I was his favourite teacher, and his father came to meet with me. We talked about his performance in school, his progress, and how he was succeeding in his studies. His father only communicated in English, and he was impressed with me and my fluency in the English language.

He asked me about my education. When I told him that I was in my second year of college working towards my bachelor's degree in commerce and accounting, he became excited. He owned a security firm that was a subsidiary of an American security firm, and his company was looking for an accountant. He offered me a great job package and salary right on the spot. I wanted to say yes, but I knew my father wouldn't allow me to work in an office environment. So, I declined his offer that same day. He still asked me to give it some thought.

When I came home, my mother told me that my father was going away to the Middle East for two years. I wasn't expecting this news as it wasn't common for him to do this sort of thing. As children, we weren't allowed to participate in our elders' conversations or have anything to say in their decisions. When I heard that he was going away for two years, I was super excited because I wanted to work for that security firm.

The next day at school, I gave a note to the child to give to his father, which read, "I have considered your offer, and if it is still available, I will be pleased to take it, but I will need a pick-up and drop-off from my home." I didn't want our driver to drive me. I was planning to lie to my mother and tell her that I was transferred to another branch of my school, and now I had transportation. I knew she would never find out.

So, I started working at this accounting firm. I was happy in this place. I had my own office space. I felt like those empowered women in English movies and some local, modern TV shows.

For outsiders looking in, my life was pretty much in control. No one would have thought that deep in my heart, I was lost and broken. The church scene was like a beautiful memory that I cherished in the deepest corners of my heart. I often thought about what it would be like to be in the church all the time. What would it be like to live as a Christian? But I immediately rebuked those thoughts and promised myself that I would never become a Christian. Yet, the longing to know about Jesus Christ was increasing with every passing day.

CHAPTER 12

THE SEA HOUSE

It was 1997. Things were still the same at home. I went to work. I went to college. I came home. I pretended to pray on my praying mat while daydreaming about church. I slept, woke up, and repeated the process, day after day.

I never had a friendly relationship with my mother. We rarely talked, except about important things. So, she didn't realize what was happening. She thought I was busy teaching and studying. I was getting better at lying. I always had an excuse for some exam to write, or paper to grade, or a meeting to attend at the school. I wonder now if she ever believed me or if she just wasn't that interested in what was happening in my life.

One day I went to work as usual. My driver picked me up and dropped me at my security firm. I told my mother I would be late because I had a parent-teacher meeting at my school. She had no clue I hadn't been working at the school for the past few months. Everything was exactly the way I wanted it to be.

When I reached my office, my boss called me into his office and said, "Rose, you are going to the Sea House today. It is temporary. Our security officer didn't show up. We are trying to find her, but she is unreachable. This client is very, very, very (emphasis on how important the client is) important for us, and they need someone fluent in English like you. So, you are going there."

I heard about the Sea House from a friend's brother a few weeks before. He had suggested that I apply for a job there. He said I would be a good fit as I was smart and spoke good English. He knew that I wanted to travel and become an air hostess. So, he encouraged me to try to get into the Sea House, but I wasn't interested in going. I liked my small office. I didn't want to do something that would reveal my lie to my family. So, when my boss asked me to go to the Sea House. I protested.

"Can you send someone else? I have reports to run today and a lot of books to balance." I lied.

"Don't worry about them. You can take your register with you and work from there to balance them. Mr. Sabir will take care of the rest here. I really want you to go there. I have no one else, and I don't want to lose our clients," he responded sternly.

Mr. Sabir was my senior accountant, and I resented him. He always tried to preach to me about how to dress like a good Muslim girl while constantly staring at my chest. He made me feel uncomfortable, and my mission was to somehow kick him out of his thirty-five-year-old job.

I didn't want to go, but I had no choice. I sensed my boss wasn't in a mood to negotiate. "Okay, I will go, but for how long do I have to be there?"

"I don't know. Maybe a week or two or until we find someone else," he responded. So, I begrudgingly agreed. I was angry at him, but I had no choice. I loved my job and didn't want to upset him. So, I collected my stuff and went to the Sea House.

CHAPTER 13

THE CHRISTIANS

I had heard a lot about this state-of-the-art, brand-new, multi-million dollar building owned by one of the largest oil and gas companies in the world. When I reached the Sea House, I was amazed at the building's size with its many levels and floors and the systems it had. A large compound lined with security cameras surrounded the whole building. The security system was amazing and top-notch for that time. There was an army of security workers, drivers, and other staff.

When I arrived, I met with Mr. Shabbir, who oversaw the security department. He gave me a tour and showed me computer rooms, labs, cafeterias, a whole floor of security offices, and amazing alarm systems. There were many things that I had never seen before. At the dining areas, he told me about one section where most Muslims gathered to eat. He mentioned many infidels (Kafirs) working in this building and eating wherever they wanted, making all eating areas "haram" (impure). So most devout Muslims decided to have a separate section to eat. He also showed me the mosque inside the building where Muslims gathered for prayer, especially on Fridays. It was an amazing building. I was impressed, but I still wanted to return to my little office in that security firm.

My first few days were uneventful. People checked in with me as they arrived. I gave them passes to the building, entered them in the computer system, called appropriate individuals from their offices, and escorted visitors. It was regular, boring, work, and a lot of male visitors were more interested in knowing about me than our building. I was exhausted, and I hated this job, but the girl who was supposed to be there was nowhere to be found. Later I heard that she was a Christian. Mr. Shabir didn't like her. I never dared to ask him why.

I was almost one week into the Sea House job, and I missed my office, but my boss told me he had been unsuccessful in finding a replacement. I started noticing many foreigners visiting. Mr. Shabbir told me that most of the higher managerial staff were from the UK and Europe, and most of the secretaries and drivers were Christians.

I became excited when I heard that there were Christians here. I thought I might find someone here who would help me with my questions about Christianity and maybe help me better understand my experience in the church, but I wasn't sure who or what to ask. I didn't know what to do, but God had already planned everything.

It happened that God gave me the opportunity to talk to someone, a Christian, on one Friday afternoon, and that became the most important conversation of my life.

CHAPTER 14

THE FRIDAY

On Fridays, no one was supposed to be in the hallway during Jumma prayer time between 12:00 and 2:00 p.m. People were supposed to go either to the mosque or stay in their offices. As a security officer, it was my job to ensure that no one was roaming around the hallways, especially in front of the mosque.

On that Friday, everything went as usual. At twelve o'clock, some people left for lunch. And some people left for the day. I was doing what I was supposed to do. Everything looked normal. Just after noon, I saw a guy walking up and down in the building. He was going in front of the mosque, then to the cafeteria, and then back to the hallway. I was bothered by him there, so I decided to find out why he wasn't in the mosque with people performing prayers. When he came behind my area, I called him to my desk.

I asked him, "Why aren't you in the mosque?"

"I am not a Muslim," he responded. "I am a Christian."

"Well, when I don't want to pray, I say I am a Christian, too. So go back to the mosque or go to your office," I said unpleasantly.

"No, seriously, I am a Christian. My dad is a pastor." He tried to convince me as if I knew what a pastor was.

"What is a pastor?" I asked. I had never heard that term before.

"A pastor is a preacher. We have a church." He answered.

"What church? Is he a father?" I said.

I only knew about the Catholic Church and priests and nuns.

"Yes, yes, like a father," he replied, smiling cheek to cheek.

I was even more confused. His dad was a priest, but fathers are celibate? I only knew Catholic Christianity at that time.

"He is a father?" I asked him, confused. "But how? How is he your father then? Don't you know that fathers don't get married?" I doubted him and wanted to share my knowledge of Catholicism with him since he was clearly lying to me about being a Christian. I was convinced he had no idea about Christianity.

"No, no, Catholic priests don't get married. My father is a pastor. Pastors can get married. We are Pentecostals." He tried to explain this, but I was even more confused and frustrated.

Now, what the heck is a Pentecostal? I had never heard this term either. I had no idea what he was talking about. I wasn't even able to say Pentecostal at that time. So, when he saw that I was confused, he started explaining how Christianity also has denominations.

"Wait, wait, does your father preach about Jesus?" I interrupted. Whatever he was telling me wasn't making any sense.

"Yes," he replied.

"Can you take me to him?" I asked.

"What?" he said.

"Can you take me to him?" I asked again.

"Why?" he asked.

"I want to know about Jesus," I answered.

He didn't respond right away and told me he was getting late and would let me know later.

I waited for his call the whole day, but he didn't call me back. I went home thinking about him and this new information about Christians. So apparently, Catholics aren't the only Christians. I couldn't wait for the office to be opened on Monday.

CHAPTER 15

CONVINCING AND CONVICTION

On Monday, when I went back to work, I realized I hadn't written his name anywhere. There were hundreds of employees in the building. Some of them had key cards and used employee entrances in the basement. I hardly saw them. I had no idea who he was and if I would ever find him.

Anyone without a key card (or contractors or visitors) had to go through security screening with me before entering. I was hoping to see him again. It was around 10:00 a.m. when I finally saw him. I was happy to see him. As he came to get his card, I smiled and whispered that he never called me on Friday, and I was waiting for his call.

He pretended that he didn't hear me because Mr. Shabbir was sitting next to me observing as I was talking to him. When I asked him again why he didn't call me, he told me he would call. As soon as he went to his office, he called me and told me that he felt uncomfortable responding in front of Mr. Shabir. I wasn't sure what he meant, but later I realized it was very dangerous for him to talk to me in a friendly way about taking me to his church in front of Mr. Shabir. Christians can often get beaten or killed for offering to help Muslims.

He didn't ask his father about taking me to his church. I now knew his name and extension number. I was happy that he wasn't a temporary worker or a contractor. He was a permanent staff member. So, from then on, I called him a few times a day and tried to talk to him about Jesus. But every time I tried to talk about Christianity, he would change the topic or hang up on me.

This went on for a couple of weeks, and I was getting frustrated. Why wasn't he taking me to his father or answering my questions? I wasn't aware of the danger I was putting him in by calling him and asking him questions about Christianity. After meeting him, my interest in Christianity was growing every day.

I started liking this job and made friends with another Christian girl in the office. She was a Goan Christian and used to go to "Tuesday Church." It was a Catholic church, too. Many people went to that church and had experienced healings and other miracles. I started to go regularly, but the father was never available to talk when I went—the desire to know Jesus was growing in my heart.

Finally, after weeks of asking him, my coworker said he would take me to his father's church, and his father was willing to answer my questions.

CHAPTER 16

THE STEEL GLASS

I had to lie to my mother about the day we planned to go to church. I told her my school had a trip somewhere, so I'd be returning home late. She believed me. I dressed up nicely and was excited to meet a 'pastor father' who could answer my questions about Jesus Christ.

After a long journey by car, rickshaw, bus, and foot, we reached a part of the city that I had never visited. We walked for an hour through winding, narrow streets, and I remember naked children playing outside in the dirt. There were heaps of garbage everywhere. We crossed a big, open sewer line covered in garbage bags. The stench coming from that open sewer line was unbearable. There were cows and goats in the middle of the streets. I wasn't sure where we were going. I was scared but determined. I wanted to meet his 'pastor father.' I wanted to know about Jesus.

After walking for an hour, he stopped at a very small home and knocked on the door. He told me that this was his cousin's home. They greeted me and took me inside. A little girl was sitting on the dirt floor trying to start a fire in a small, handmade fire pit made of a few bricks. She was cooking dinner for me.

As a Muslim, a few years earlier, I would have hated to take anything from a Christian's hand. I would have never thought to eat in a Christian home, a meal prepared by a Christian girl in their own dishes. It would have been unimaginable, but that day was different.

She served me a rice and chickpeas dinner on a steel plate and a glass of cold water in a steel glass. As I took the glass from her hand, I remembered something from my home. At the bottom of our sink, next to our trash can, we kept exactly the same glass. It was for our sweeper. No one was allowed to touch that glass except our servant, Mustafa. Even he picked it up with great caution so he wouldn't touch the actual utensil because it would make him unclean.

When I thought about it, I felt a big lump in my throat. I was drinking water given to me by a Christian girl from a similar steel glass. I was eating food prepared by her hands. I was eating and drinking from dishes used by these Christians. And I desired to live with these Christians for the rest of my life. I desired not to return to my home but to stay with them and make them my family. I desired to call them my own.

I quietly finished my food, returned her plate, and thanked her for her hospitality.

CHAPTER 17

VISIT TO A CHURCH

After we were done eating, our journey started again. We walked for another thirty minutes. By that time, it was getting dark. I couldn't recognize any of the streets. I was still thinking about that little girl who cooked for me and served me. I was thinking about her brick stove, steel glass and plate, her food, and for some reason, my eyes were welling up with tears. I felt so much love for that girl. I didn't understand. The rest of our journey was very quiet.

After walking in the dark for a while, we stopped in front of a white door. Outside I saw the nameplate "Sameer Masih. B.Th." He rang the bell, and my heart stopped beating for a few seconds. I felt like I had waited my whole life for this moment.

His father answered the door. The first thing his father did was lay his hands on my head and say, "Bless you, my daughter." Then he invited me to their humble, two-room house. One was a bedroom, and another was a living room. I was led to the living room.

As I looked around, I noticed a small bed in the living room and a grey cupboard adorned with Bible verse stickers. There was a sofa, a small bookcase, and a small table like a study table. On the study table, there was a thick, black-covered book with words in silver written on it, "Kitab-e-Muqaddas" (the Holy Book). It was the first time that I laid my eyes on the Bible. My heart raced within me. I was in a Christian home. He said it was a church, but it was a home. Every pore of my body was sweating. I was scared, joyful, and nervous.

It was the first time I saw and met Christians who were not Catholics. The church was a house, or the house was a church. I just saw the Bible in the house. I forgot about all my questions. This wasn't anything like the concept of Christianity I had in my mind.

After I sat down, his father said prayers before we began our conversation. The first question I asked him was why they were not like Catholics? Why did they not have big cathedrals or any statues of Mother Mary or Jesus in their house?

His father then explained it to me, but it didn't make any sense back then. I don't remember what else we talked about, but I clearly remember that I didn't want to go back to my home that night. I wanted to stay there and touch that black-covered Bible. I wanted to see the inside. I wanted to know what the Bible taught about Islam and Mohammed and especially about Jesus Christ. But I couldn't gather my strength to ask him to see the Bible, and it was almost too late to stay there, so I asked them to take me back home. That night I couldn't sleep well.

The next day, when I went to work, I called him several times and asked him many questions. In my zeal to know more about Christianity, I didn't realize I was jeopardizing his safety and that of his family. I didn't know Mr. Shabbir was listening to all my calls.

CHAPTER 18

LUNCH HOUR EVANGELISM

After visiting his home and meeting his father and family, I couldn't wait any longer to know more about Jesus Christ. I had been waiting for four years for someone to tell me about Jesus, and here I was sitting in this strange house church—for the first time in my life, I had laid my eyes on the Bible. I saw the Bible. The Bible that we were told was lost. I saw it. It was within my reach.

Every day, I had so many questions about the Bible and Jesus Christ. The first time I touched the Bible, I remember I could hear my heart beating in my chest a hundred times faster. As I grabbed the Bible and put it respectfully on the pillow I had on my lap, I stared at the black cover for a few seconds in disbelief. I had touched the Bible.

When my friend saw my zeal and realized that I was genuinely serious about Christianity, he took me to one of his missionary friends whose wife was a convert from Islam. Obviously, I had no idea about her conversion at that time. Only very trustworthy people were sent to this missionary couple.

Muslims used to disguise themselves as seekers and spy on Christians involved in evangelism. Those ministering to Muslim seekers were in great danger, and they still are. It is a dangerous thing to minister to a Muslim.

In most Islamic nations, proselytizing is strictly forbidden and punishable by death. Those who are caught distributing Christian literature or sharing the gospel with Muslims meet with severe beatings, jail time, and can even be sentenced to death under the blasphemy law. I wasn't aware of all this danger.

As a Muslim, I was taught to hate Christians and Jews but never thought of the circumstances most Christians lived in every day. I was just excited that someone would now teach me about Jesus. This couple was helping people like me who were lost and searching for truth at the cost of their lives. I loved going to their home and learning about Jesus.

Every day, for a few months during lunchtime, we visited them. They answered my questions about Jesus Christ and Christianity. They even answered my questions about Islam, Mohammed, and all that had kept me awake for many countless nights.

After five months of studying under them, I finally decided to give my life to the Lord Jesus Christ. I knew it would be extremely dangerous for both the friend who helped me and for me. I knew I could lose everything, even my life, but I wanted to follow Jesus at any cost.

I wanted to be baptized, so on the shores of the Indian Ocean one crisp March morning, I was baptized. I died that day with Christ and rose again as part of His bride.

CHAPTER 19

The Marriage

After I gave my life to the Lord Jesus Christ, I couldn't live as a Muslim. I didn't know how to tell my family. I didn't want to live in my parents' home anymore. I wanted to be with my real family—my Christian family.

Above all, I wanted to own a Bible, which wasn't possible if I continued living at my parents' home. But I had no choice. After I was baptized, I went back to work and my home, and I lived outwardly as a Muslim.

One day I heard my father had abruptly left the Middle East and returned. I was now scared. If he found out about my conversion and work in the office, he would kill me, so I tried to continue to lie.

I had a childhood friend I helped get a job at the security firm where I worked. She was the third wife of a man almost fifty years older than her. He used to beat her, but she was a devout Muslim woman. Despite her miserable life, she always prayed and asked me to perform prayers regularly. I often talked with her about my doubts and fears about Islam. She was the one who encouraged me to go to temples and monks.

Ever since I got involved in Christianity, I had been less interested in talking to her. One day she told me that Mr. Shabbir had called her and told her that I was involved with some Christian people in my office. I didn't lie, and I told her that I'd been checking out Christianity, but I hid the details about my baptism and Bible study. She then mentioned that my family was planning my marriage with my cousin. When I heard about this, I became very scared. I knew if I got married to my cousin, I would never be able to follow Christianity.

I shared this news with my pastors, and on their recommendation, my Christian friend and I decided to get married.

I don't know how, but everything got arranged, and I quietly took vows in front of the pastor and a lawyer with my Christian friend. His family wasn't happy about this decision because they feared my family. After we signed our marriage register, we came back to work. It happened during lunchtime.

We decided to continue to work and save money until we had enough to leave the country. That was our plan, but God had a different plan for us.

The day we got married, I told my friend about it. It was my biggest mistake. I thought she would hide it from my parents like she hid many other things, but she didn't. She took the rest of the day off from work and went to my home. I didn't know about her intentions. When I reached home, I saw her leaving my house, and my mother was crying. My father was looking furious. I knew she had told my parents about me. I had nowhere to escape.

As my father saw me, he approached me and asked, "Is what Shazia told us true? Did you become a Christian? Did you marry a Christian man?"

All the blood in my veins froze. I had no idea how I responded, but I remember saying in a faint voice, "Yes, I did."

The moment those words left my mouth, my father lifted me up from the ground and threw me against the wall. I hit my head on the wall and became unconscious. When I gained consciousness, I found myself locked in a room. I tried to go outside and knocked on the door, but no one responded. I was in a very dark and difficult place, alone with nowhere to turn to. I was scared. I had no idea how long I was there. I had no one to talk to. But I felt a big burden had been lifted. Now my parents knew.

CHAPTER 20

THE IMPRISONMENT

I wasn't sure what day it was. I hadn't changed clothes in weeks, and I reeked. Sometimes they forgot to give me food. Wondering what my father would do next was driving me insane. Every time he came in, he asked: "Who helped you become a Christian? Do you want to live? Then, recant Christianity and accept Islam."

I didn't learn how to pray properly, so I talked to Jesus and told Him everything.

"Jesus, You know what happened today. I don't want to respond to my father, but my silence aggravates him. He beats me with sticks. I didn't think he would ever beat me. My mother isn't listening to me either. She says things that no one should say to their daughter. My sisters, oh, I love them so much, and they call me a whore. Jesus, where are you? Help me."

Every day, I used to pray like this. I didn't know anything else. I memorized the Lord's Prayer, which was the only piece of the Bible I had with me in my heart. No one was talking to me. I was locked in this barely furnished room used by our servants. I wasn't sure if I would ever make it out alive.

My father had a routine. First thing in the morning and before bed, he would come and ask those questions. He used his cane to beat me when I answered negatively. This went on for about a month.

Then one day, he came in furious, threatening to kill me if I didn't accept Islam and identify who helped me. My silence only added to his anger. He beat me until he broke his cane. I cried the entire night with pain in my back.

The next day he threatened to send me to the Northern Province of my country where my uncle lived, a province that is under strict Sharia law. I believed I would be killed if I went. I had no one to talk to in that small room. It was only Jesus and me.

After a couple of months, my father visited again. It seemed like he had suddenly grown very old. Instead of hatred, I felt compassion for him. I started to silently recite the Lord's Prayer. He told me this was his last warning. If I wanted freedom, I must reveal who helped me and recant Christianity. Instead of saying no to him, I started reciting the Lord's Prayer louder.

When he heard me saying the words, he didn't understand, but he got furious. He went outside and came back with a big knife. As my father approached, my younger sister ran through the hallway screaming, "Help, something happened to mother." There was screaming and wailing in the main building. My father quickly left to find out what had happened. My mother was having a heart attack. He left to take her to the hospital.

After he left, my younger sister came and told me what had happened. She begged me to listen to my father. She took me to her room, and I had my first bath in weeks and was able to change into clean clothes.

I finally saw my brothers and sisters. They hugged me and we all started crying bitterly. I felt so much love and compassion for them. I felt like my heart was going to explode with pain. They all begged me to come back to Islam and listen to my father. I told them I couldn't do that. Then they started cursing me. They forced me back into the room. They were younger than me. My youngest brother was only six years old, and I loved them so much, but at that moment, I realized that I loved Jesus more.

I didn't know much about the Bible. I didn't know the verses about whoever loves their family more than me is not worthy of me. I didn't know about the Beatitudes.

It was another difficult day, and I had to choose—my family or my faith—and I chose Jesus (or He chose me). I decided to remain in Christ even if it would cost my life.

CHAPTER 21

ATTEMPTED SUICIDE

When I was changing clothes in my sister's room, I stole some of her traditional glass jewellery, planning to crush the glass and end my life. I didn't want to leave Jesus or my family. I didn't want to deny Jesus or hurt my family either. I thought of the ultimate solution—if I died, I would be in heaven with Jesus, and my family wouldn't have to face shame. But God was planning something else.

After things quieted down and my parents returned home, one night I decided to eat the crushed glass. I don't remember what happened as I was rendered unconscious, but I woke up in the hospital. I saw my mother sleeping on the couch. I was hooked up with IVs. I didn't know how I survived my attempted suicide.

I was disappointed, but I had no choice but to live. My mother stayed with me 24/7. She often cried, sometimes loudly, sometimes quietly, begging me to have mercy on her and our family.

I would watch her on her prayer mat, sitting and crying bitterly. She lost interest in eating and became quiet and sad. Seeing her like this shattered my heart into pieces. I loved her so much, but I loved Jesus more. I wanted to comfort her, but I didn't know how.

One day my father came to the hospital to visit me. He had a doctor's note in his hand, which said that I was mentally unstable and tried to take my life. So, this would work in his favour if he decided to kill me. But he told me that he had chosen my punishment. He would marry me off to my cousin in the Northern Province.

I was terrified and longed for death. Although I considered myself married to my friend, this meant nothing in Islam. That day I cried constantly and asked Jesus to reveal Himself. I was at the end of my rope and wanted Jesus to appear to me and comfort me, and He did.

CHAPTER 22

THE CROSSROAD

I'm not sure if it was a dream or a vision, but I saw myself standing at a crossroads. The road on one side led to a church, and the other road led to a mosque. The road to the church was broken and deserted. It looked difficult to walk on, but the road leading to the mosque was beautiful, nicely landscaped, and felt desirable. I stood at the crossroads in confusion, wondering which road to take. Then I heard a voice—"Close your eyes and spin seven times. Open your eyes on the seventh spin and choose the road that is before your eyes." I did this, and after my seventh spin, I opened my eyes—the road that led to the church was in front of me.

I started walking on that broken road. As I took my first steps, I heard my mother's voice calling me, asking me to go back. She told me I had made a mistake and that my family was at the back waiting for me. Ignoring her voice, I continued my walk. As I drew closer to the church, I heard wailing and mourning in the background as in a funeral.

I heard my mother screaming and cursing at me. Then her voice changed to something scary and demonic, threatening to kill me, but I continued my journey. After a long, tiresome journey, I reached the church door. It was a beautiful, big, cathedral-style church door. I knocked at the door, and a person answered. I didn't know who this was. It was a man wearing white clothes, shining like a light. The light was so bright that I was unable to see his face. He put his hand on my head and said these words "My daughter, you are saved, and you have received salvation."

As soon as he finished speaking, I woke from this vision. I felt like I had walked a million miles and was drenched in sweat. There was bright daylight outside. I looked at my mother, and I saw her sleeping soundly. Her veil was lying beside her on the floor.

CHAPTER 23

THE FINAL ESCAPE

As I thought about the dream or vision I'd just had, I felt that God was giving me the opportunity to escape. I gathered my strength, hid in my mother's veil (Burqa) and left the room, locking it from the outside behind me. I quickly went outside, where the taxi drivers waited for customers. I sat in the first taxi I saw and told him to take me to a place that my pastor had told me to go in case of an emergency or something like this.

The taxi driver knew that area well, so he took me there. It was two hours away from the hospital on the other side of the city. As I reached this area, I asked the taxi driver to wait for me outside on the street. The streets in this area were narrow and broken. Cars, taxis, and rickshaws couldn't enter there. I told him my brother would bring his fare, which was a normal practice back then.

I finally reached my husband's friend's house and sent him back to the taxi, but the driver had already left. He called my husband and set up a place for us to meet. The next morning, I finally saw my husband after several months. He looked scared, and we left our city that day and went to another province a thousand miles away.

CHAPTER 24

ON THE RUN

My husband told me that he knew something must have been wrong when he didn't see me at work the next day. Thankfully, his Christian friends worked as telephone operators in the Sea House. They told him that they had erased our conversations because someone was asking them for the recordings of the calls between us.

My father's men were coming to the Sea House to find out who helped in my conversion. So, my husband had to leave his job after a few weeks when I didn't show up. By then, they established that I must have been imprisoned or killed as I hadn't spoken to anyone in my office or the outside world for weeks.

He also told me that some Muslims came to his street, inquiring about me. They threw stones at Christian homes and went from home to home asking about me. It was a difficult situation for him, but God protected him. He was sent to live with another friend in a different part of the city.

The entire Christian community on his street was alert. At any time, anything could have happened. Not many people knew about us. We kept my conversion and our marriage hidden. So, when my father's people asked people in the community, no one knew about us. When his friend contacted him to say that I was at his home, he didn't believe it because he thought I was dead.

So, moving to another province, for the time being, was our only option. My husband's family was too scared to keep me at their home because of the danger.

However, my husband's distant relatives lived in different parts of the country. So, we lived with one of his relatives for a while before moving on to another. As an ex-Muslim, it was dangerous to live in one place for a long time. For months we moved from one home to another to keep us and those giving us refuge safe.

We had no plan, no job, and no money. There was no support from our families. We didn't know what our future would be like. We lived one day at a time, trusting God. I can't remember how many sleepless nights we had. When we woke up, we prayed. When things died down a little bit, we returned to my husband's parents' home. We lived in a small room where his grandparents used to live. We made our temporary home in that room, knowing that we might have to leave at a moment's notice.

I spent most of my days reading the Bible, absorbing as much as I could. I finished reading the entire Bible in a few months. As a new believer, I thought reading and reciting the Bible was important and would make God happy.

I don't remember where I found the Bible-study material, but I started doing these long-distance Bible courses. I used to get the courses through some church people, and once I finished them, they would provide me with another one to do. It was time for me to grow in my faith, and God made it possible for me to understand the Bible. I discovered a whole new world in the Bible, and the more I studied it, the more I loved it. I think this was the beginning of my theological studies.

Even though our lives were tough with no house, money, or jobs, we were happy. We had enormous support from our larger Christian community. During this time, I became pregnant, and we had our first daughter. I went unregistered to a charity hospital when my water broke. I gave birth, and within two hours, I left the hospital with a newborn baby. There was no medicine, epidurals, or birthing exercises. I barely had food to eat during my pregnancy, but God kept us safe and gave me the strength to deliver her and leave the hospital right away.

As we held our daughter in our hands, for the first time, we felt fear. What if someone kidnapped her or forcefully converted her to Islam? The fear of such an unknown future shook the very core of our beings. We didn't know where we would live or what kind of life we would give our children, but we had trust in God. We were at peace, knowing that whatever happened, God would be in the middle of it.

CHAPTER 25

THE PASSPORTS

After the birth of our daughter, my husband and I became serious about leaving our country. We knew it would be hard to leave, and we looked for options. My husband had many friends settled in different countries. In fact, one of his uncles was an important Christian minister who travelled to Europe and North America often, but we didn't receive any help from him. I was surprised that someone in a position to help would withhold it, especially a Christian pastor.

Slowly, I realized that Christians weren't perfect. There were fights, jealousy, and gossip among them. Most of them struggled with sin just like anyone else, but there was a big difference. The sinning Christian can repent, put his sin on Jesus, and trust Him for forgiveness. But a Muslim must work hard to remove the stains of sin and even present a blood sacrifice year after year to Allah, who might forgive their sins. They have no assurance of forgiveness.

Anyway, we were quite disheartened when his uncle refused to help. Access to any information was only through television or newspaper. The Internet hadn't been invented, and computers weren't common in my country. We had no idea how to leave or where to go.

Still, we were told by many wise people in our church to get our passports just in case. It wasn't easy for us to get passports because we had no money, and they were expensive. In addition, I had no legal documents, and everything was done manually by hand back then.

To obtain a passport, you had to go to the passport office and present your birth certificate and the required documents, which I didn't have. Even if you did everything right, it was a hundred times harder for a Christian to obtain a passport than a Muslim due to discrimination and segregation. We heard stories about how Christians were treated at these government offices, and the only way to make it work was to bribe the officers.

But we needed passports to escape our country. My husband's aunt used to work in a government office. Finally, she pulled some strings, and we obtained our passports. Although my birth certificate was required, she somehow listed me as an orphan and used my husband's first name as my last name on the application. She paid the officer a bribe, and we received our passports.

I still remember the day we held our passports in our hands. It felt like we had achieved a great milestone. Passports were the keys to unlock the door for our travels. Now, all we had to do was find a country we could easily go to, and we wanted to go to a Christian country.

CHAPTER 26

THE DIVINE PROVIDENCE

We had our passports but didn't know where we could go. Every country's entry requirements were tough. We didn't have enough money, education, or skills to travel to Europe or other places.

The Internet had just been introduced, and only rich people could afford it. My husband's sister started a job in an Internet-providing company. She told us stories about how they connected with the world. She was active in her father's church as a church secretary and sent letters and reports to their main denomination in North America and other parts of the world.

She started connecting us with some Christian missionaries in the outside world. Some of these missionaries had visited our country to do crusades and seminars through my father-in-law's church. They were willing to help us, but it wasn't easy to get visas for any developed country. She was also trying to find a way out of our birth country, just like every other Christian.

One day she registered my husband on an American website for Christian pen pals. It was through this website that we were able to connect with a missionary working in Japan. After hearing about our situation, he offered to help us.

We made several Christian friends through this website. All of them were Christians from North America. But two people, in particular, became very important in our lives. God used them mightily, and to this day, we are grateful for their love, friendship, help, and support.

One of them became my lifelong sister, and through her, God filled the vacuum I had when I left my family and sisters. She supported us in every possible way. Currently, she lives in New Jersey and has a family of her own. After we arrived in Canada, she visited us and became my children's aunt.

It was a miracle how two people living thousands of miles away were willing to help a couple in a third-world country they had never visited. But our God is a God of miracles. He already made the way for us. We just had to wait patiently for His plan to unfold.

When we shared with our friend that we could go anywhere if it was a Christian country, he introduced us to his friends in Africa. And we prepared to go to Africa.

CHAPTER 27

THE AIRPORT

We reached the nearest international airport. As I stepped out of the van with a dozen church members, I realized I was shaking, scared, and nervous. I felt like all eyes were on me. Every pore of my body was sweating. I was scared—would they let us board the plane? What if they sent us to prison? What if they took our little girl from us?

As we approached customs, they started asking questions. "Where are you going?"

"Uganda," my husband responded.

"Do you have a visa?"

"Yes, see this." He showed them our visas.

"Is she your wife?"

"Yes," my husband responded.

I was scared and didn't make eye contact. I hid my face behind my daughter so that he couldn't see me clearly. My throat was dry. I felt I had "Apostate. Capture her, kill her and kill her husband too," written all over my face.

I was silently praying, calling upon the name of Jesus. As he opened our luggage and started going through our stuff, my heart sank. I had put a couple of Bibles in my luggage. He picked up my "Good News" English Bible with a red cover, flipped through the pages and put it back. Even though our passports listed our religion as "Christians," I was still scared that they would find out that I wasn't born a Christian. But nothing happened.

After an hour of checking our stuff, documents, and further questioning (answered mainly by my husband), we were cleared to go to the gate and board our plane. I couldn't believe it. We were soon going to board our plane and leave our birth country behind. It was all like a dream. I was so scared of missing our plane that I didn't even go to the bathroom.

We waited for an hour at our gate before our plane opened for boarding. My husband and I were praying the entire time. Finally, the boarding gate opened. Because we had a baby, we were allowed to board with the first-class passengers. We sat in the plane in our designated seats though I still wasn't satisfied. We were still in my city. Until our plane climbed in the air, we held onto each other tightly, silently praying.

Once we were flying and the captain announced our destination landing time, we breathed our first sigh of relief. I told my husband, "I can't believe we are really leaving our birth country," and we both said a prayer of thanksgiving.

Although we were happy to be free, we were sad to leave our loved ones behind, especially my husband's family. It was the best day of our lives because we were moving towards our freedom, but it was also a sad day because we knew we might never return to our birth country.

CHAPTER 28

THE PEARL OF AFRICA

After several transfers of planes and airports, we landed at Entebbe in Uganda. As the plane was landing, we saw the majestic, beautiful Lake Victoria surrounded by small hills and red earth. A few days before our trip, I dreamed of a beautiful big lake surrounded by red earth. I drew the image in my journal and showed it to my husband the following day.

As he was looking down from the plane's window, he screamed with excitement, "Hey, look! This is exactly like the drawing you made in your journal after your dream." We knew right then that this is where God would keep us and give us freedom.

Our plane touched the ground. As we exited the plane, we breathed the fresh air of freedom for the first time. Finally, we were free. There was no fear of my father's people capturing us here. After we cleared through customs, we were welcomed at the VIP lounge by our friends, who came to pick us up.

We were taken to the home of a Scottish lady, Roberta. She'd been living there as a missionary for some time. She prepared delicious Scottish beef stew for us, the most delicious meal we'd had in a very long time. After eating, we thanked God for our safe arrival and shared our stories with our new Ugandan family. Finally, after midnight, we said goodnight to each other and went to our room, where our beds were neatly made.

I couldn't sleep at all the entire night. I was excited, relieved, happy, and at the same time, uncertain about what our future would be in this new land.

CHAPTER 29

IN A STRANGE LAND

On our first morning in Uganda, I woke up early. It was a little chilly in our room. I peeked through the window and saw a beautiful sight in Roberta's backyard. She had many trees in her green backyard, and beautiful birds were perched on them, singing their morning songs.

I had never seen such beautiful birds.

There was an abundance of avocado, pineapple, jackfruit, mango, and banana trees. The soil was red, rich, and fertile. The night before, it had rained, and I could see the mist rising from the earth and droplets on the leaves.

Back home, we barely had any grass or fruit trees. We had sparrows and crows and maybe a pigeon here or there. But here, in Roberta's backyard, my eyes witnessed something beautiful. Red, little birds, coloured-feathered birds, big birds, small birds, all busy singing a song of praise to our Lord, or at least that was what I thought they were doing.

After a while, everyone woke up, and Roberta called us for breakfast. After eating, it was time for our host to introduce us to his church. Roberta lived near a slum but had a nice house. As I was getting ready, I put on my long skirt and blouse. For the first time, I didn't have to worry about covering my face. I realized I was truly free.

That day our host showed us many things in the neighbourhood. We enjoyed an amazing worship time with our Ugandan church family. We went to the market to get diapers and milk for our daughter. He showed us how to take a boda boda (motorcycle taxi). It was one of the days of my life that I'll never forget. For the first time, I truly felt free. No one was watching me or coming after me. We found many new friends and family in the Ugandan church and enjoyed every moment of our days there.

CHAPTER 30

THE APARTMENT

After staying for a couple of weeks at Roberta's home, we found a nice apartment on top of a house owned by an army major. We moved into this apartment, which we shared with another local person. We still didn't know how long we would live here, but slowly we furnished our new home.

I remember somebody gave us couches without cushions. We had to put cardboard boxes on the wood for seating, but we were happy. Our kitchen had a nice stove. We were given a set of dishes with a dinner set. It was all we needed. We were happy. We had a place to live and call home, or so we thought.

We didn't know the complications of immigration or anything else. We trusted God for our tomorrows like little children. The person who helped us get our visas was an ex-immigration officer who became a pastor. He was trying to extend our visas, but there were some complications because we didn't have enough money to extend the visas. Our friend supporting us just lost his job, and we had no way of supporting ourselves as we were on missionary visas. But we trusted the Lord, and He knew what He was doing.

CHAPTER 31

CONNECTIONS MADE BY GOD

My husband somehow got a small bump on his thigh. We didn't know what it was, but it was growing. We thought he should see the doctor and get it checked. There was a small hospital on our street. On the day he went there, he saw a Christian nurse who was also a missionary who had lived in Uganda for many years. She was originally from Scotland. Soon they started talking, and she was delighted to hear that we knew Roberta. She invited us to the birthday party of her friend's son, and my husband accepted.

When we went to the birthday party, we met a Christian family from our country. We were so happy to find each other—they hadn't met anyone from the same country in a long time. They had been living in Uganda for five years as refugees, waiting to resettle in the USA.

When they heard about our situation, they told us about the asylum process. We had never even heard the word asylum and had no idea about the refugee process. We didn't understand much that day, so they agreed to meet with us the next day.

They picked us up in their truck early the next morning and took us to their home. They were living in a guest house as the Church of Uganda was helping them. They explained the process in detail and promised to take us to the office to file our case.

Although we had no idea about this procedure, we knew one thing for sure. We didn't want to go back to our country. After discussing it with our friend Roberta and our ex-immigration officer friend, we decided to give it a try.

They took us to the office the next day, where we filed our application as asylum seekers. We didn't know what that meant, but we knew God was leading us.

CHAPTER 32

BECOMING STATELESS

A s we sat in the office waiting for our turn for an interview, we saw a long line of people outside the door. The line extended to the other side of the street. Some of them had little children. Some of them looked sick and malnourished. As I looked at them, I asked the clerk who all these people were. He answered in a serious tone that they were refugees. They were all waiting in line to meet with someone, hoping to get some good news. I felt intimidated by him and didn't dare ask him any further questions.

But I had so many questions—such as, why did they need refugee status? Weren't they all living here? Weren't they all Ugandans? I didn't know that millions of people sought refuge in Uganda from Rwanda and Somalia.

We were sitting in the UNHCR office, but we didn't know that this was the office providing help for refugees. We were so young and naive. We had no idea that worldwide millions of people become refugees every day due to wars, conflicts, poverty, and terrorism. We didn't know what we were getting ourselves into.

A few moments later, we were called in for an interview. I held my daughter tightly to my chest, and we all went into the office. An imposing white man was sitting behind the desk. He directed us to sit in some chairs. He looked serious as he read through some papers in the file folder he was holding. We sat quietly. My heart was beating a hundred miles an hour. We didn't know what to say.

After a few minutes of silence, he looked at us and started asking us questions.

"What is your name?" he asked me directly—this time I had to respond.

"Tell me from the start what happened to you and why you don't want to return to your country?" Again, the question was directed to me.

I could hear my voice cracking. I told him everything, how I was beaten and tortured for leaving Islam and how I had to escape, how we had to live in hiding and sometimes without food. He listened to my whole story without interrupting.

As soon as I finished, he took some papers from the file folder, signed them, and gave them to his secretary to stamp. We still didn't know what was going on.

Then he returned to his desk and told us his secretary would give us our documents. He approved our application for asylum, and now we could live and work in Uganda until they could find us a sponsor. He told us many things, but we only remembered the part where he said we could "live and work in Uganda freely." As his secretary handed him the documents, he walked us to the door and shook hands with us. We went home thanking God for providing us with a legal way to live in Uganda.

CHAPTER 33

GUIDANCE IN THE VISIONS

For several nights, I had a strange dream. In my dream, I saw myself standing in a room. A voice spoke to me, telling me to go to a certain hill in Kampala where there was a church and meet the bishop there. I shared the dream with my husband, but he thought it was nothing.

After a few days, I had the same dream again, and this time the voice increased its urgency that I should go and meet this bishop. I didn't tell my husband this time. I got ready in the morning, took boda boda (the motorbike taxi) and told the driver to take me to this church on a hill. I was curious to see if the driver knew if there was an actual church on a hill. To my surprise, he responded with a nod, and after ten minutes, he was driving up a hill called Namirembe Hill and taking me to the Anglican Church of Uganda.

When I was dropped off at the entrance of the church administration office, a person asked me if I was there to see the bishop. I told him yes, I was there to see the bishop. He pointed to the house on the street and asked me to go there. When I reached the house, the archbishop came out and asked me if I was there to see the bishop. He pointed me to another big house at the end of the street.

As I was walking towards the bishop's house, I was getting a little disappointed and thought maybe my husband was right.

I might be imagining things. As I reached the house, I saw a long line of people standing there to see the bishop. Seeing this increased my disappointment, but I decided to stay.

As I stood thinking about my dream, a girl approached and told me to follow her. She brought me inside and pointed me towards a room to enter. I walked into a big living room in the residence of the bishop of the Church of Uganda. The walls were adorned with pictures and Bible verses. There was a large picture of the bishop in his purple robe. I sat on one of the couches and wondered if my dream was coming true.

After a few minutes, I heard footsteps behind me and saw the bishop walking towards me. When I saw him, I stood and shook his hand. As we sat, I repeated everything about myself and my dream. After hearing my story and dream, he smiled and told me to meet him in his office. He asked me to call my husband, and then he left. He told me he was a very busy man, so we must keep the time as he had to leave soon to visit some village.

I didn't know what to make of all of this. I was left standing in the middle of that big living room, wondering. Again, doubts crept into my mind. Was I just wasting my time? But I decided to call my husband. I told him to come right away as the bishop wanted to meet him and had limited time. It was around 8:45 a.m. The bishop was supposed to lead the daily devotions for his staff at 9:00 a.m. All diocesan staff were required to join the morning devotions and prayers. Then everyone was dispersed to go to their offices. I didn't know that the bishop was asking us to join the morning devotions with his staff.

As we walked into the office with our little daughter, the bishop was leading in prayer. We sat down on the available chairs. After the prayer, the bishop asked us to come forward. As we walked to him, he put his hand on my shoulders and introduced me to his staff. He told them that God had sent them a daughter and a son.

He said he would adopt us as his children, and we would be living with him in his guest house. He also said we would be working at that office. We were dumbfounded. We had no words to explain what had just happened.

After the devotional time, he took us to his office. It was a nice, comfortable office. He called his wife and told her that he was sending their new children. Prepare the guest house for them. He then explained what we would be doing. He created a job for me, working with his project coordinator, and he asked my husband to help with networking in their newly opened centre for HIV and AIDS patients.

My husband and I had nothing to say. On that day, we got jobs, the house, and the family we stayed with until we left Uganda. I was awestruck at how God came to rescue us. It was unbelievable what God did, and for the first time, I felt the fear of the Lord. It wasn't the fear of his wrath but the bigness and greatness of his majesty. That day I realized even more that our God is a living God, and He cares about every part of our lives.

CHAPTER 34

MOVING IN AND SETTLING DOWN

We were still in disbelief about how God provided. We were given a huge house with a giant bedroom, a room for a kitchen, and a three-piece bathroom. The house, built by colonizers in the -1800s, was made of red bricks, surrounded by beautiful trees, and sat on the hill facing the city. At night, we could enjoy a view of the city of Kampala from the porch. The house was heavily guarded by armed guards as the bishop was an important person in the country. We were also given a car with a driver to do our chores. It was the safest place to live and work in Uganda, and we had the freedom to come and go as we pleased.

We both got ready early the next morning, left our daughter with a nanny provided by the diocese, and went to the office. As we walked to the church office, we praised God for this provision. We had searched for jobs for over three months, and sometimes we didn't even have enough left to buy food after paying rent. We didn't know that God had been preparing a place for us to live and work.

Our first day of work was amazing. After devotions, I was taken to my office and shown my own desk and computer. My job was fun, and I loved it. I met new people and learned every day how God was using the Church of Uganda in their lives. There were great projects and programs the Church was doing to help people.

My job was to accompany the project director and survey the areas that needed assessment. It was a humbling and life-transforming experience. I still remember the day I went to a small village surrounded by a thick forest in the middle of nowhere. Only one dirt road (which looked more like a trail) connected the village to the nearest town, which was more than a three hours' drive away.

I saw men, women, and young children carrying yellow jerry cans and walking on the side of the road as we drove. I asked my driver where they were going. He told me they walked every morning for two hours to the nearest well to get water. We were there to conduct a survey and then present a proposal to build a well near their village so they didn't have to walk so far.

When we reached the village, the priest came out to greet us. He took us to his home (which was more like a mud hut) and presented us with food and water. Everyone from the village came to meet us. I was mostly quiet as I didn't speak their language. After hearing their stories and making notes, we were ready to leave. As we sat in the truck, a person came with a basket full of eggs and gave it to me. Then another person came with a sack of potatoes, beans, a pineapple, and some other local vegetables.

I didn't know what was happening. I thought they were trying to sell me this stuff. As I was about to tell them no thank you, the driver told me that it was a custom there. These are the gifts for "muzungu" (visitors). "Muzungu" means "white" in the Luganda language. It was considered impolite to say no to the gifts. I thought these people had nothing, yet they chose to give their best to visitors. This was something clearly lacking in our society. I have so many stories to share from this amazing place; I might write another book about my experiences in Uganda.

CHAPTER 35

THE INTERVIEW AND THE FAREWELL

It was a typical day as we arrived home from work and went to pick up some dinner from one of the markets. As we were ordering food, our cell phone rang. My husband picked up his phone, and the person said something quickly, which my husband asked him to repeat.

After looking at his phone with a surprised expression, my husband grabbed my shoulders and said, "We are going to Canada. It was the officer from UNHCR. He told us we have to meet the visa officer next week for our interview. Canada has approved our application."

I couldn't believe my ears. We were going to Canada?! Really? It was great news. We knew that Uganda wasn't our permanent home, so we were happy, but we loved Uganda and our church family there.

Although we knew it was God's doing, and we were ready to move anywhere God had for us, we had mixed feelings. We shared this news with Bishop Daddy, who shared our joy.

The next week we went to see the Canadian visa officer. After asking us some questions, she asked us to sign a loan agreement, which was between the Government of Canada and us. We were sponsored directly by the government. They paid for our tickets, medical, and all expenses related to our travel. We were even more amazed at how God was taking care of our needs in a powerful way.

The day before our flight, our church friends and co-workers gave us a big farewell party. The diocese people came to say goodbye. In a few short years, they had become our family. We worked with them, worshipped with them, and lived with them. It was hard to say goodbye, but we had to leave.

Daddy Bishop's house was close to the Entebbe Airport, so they offered us his house overnight to avoid delays. After the party, we went to the bishop's home. He made pork chops for our last dinner.

The next day, he sent us off in the special fleet that he used for his personal travels. After many tears, hugs, and kisses, we said goodbye to each other. We came to Uganda with one suitcase. We left Uganda with one suitcase. God took care of our every need and provided more than we could imagine, and we knew he would take care of us. With this trust in our hearts, we boarded our plane to fly to our new homeland, Canada.

CHAPTER 36

O CANADA, OUR HOME AND NATIVE LAND!

After four plane transfers and four airports, we finally reached Toronto Pearson Airport. Peeking through the plane window, we saw the magical city of Toronto below us. The cars on the highway looked like Lego pieces. It was like a scene from a Hollywood movie. We couldn't believe that we would soon be a part of this magical landscape. The sun was shining brightly, so we assumed it would be warm. After hours of paperwork, interviews, and customs, we were allowed to enter the country.

Our Canadian missionary friends from Uganda knew about our arrival, so they offered to pick us up. They actually prepared an apartment for us. God had already arranged everything before we even arrived.

We saw our friend, Barbara, waiting for us as we walked outside. She welcomed us with a warm hug and a beautiful Canadian flower bouquet. She offered us Tim Hortons coffee and tea. She also handed us some warm coats, and we wondered because it was sunny outside. As soon as we stepped outside, we realized it was an October sun.

As she drove home, I was amazed at what I saw: beautiful roads, big cars, huge buildings, and clean air. Everything felt magical. Finally, after an hour, she pointed at a building and said, "Welcome to Canada. This is your home."

Our apartment was on top of a Christian cafe. It was a one-bedroom, very clean apartment. It was fully furnished. Our daughter had her own bed. Everything was provided for us. We just had to bring our suitcase and put clothes in the closet. That was it. I opened the fridge to discover that it already had milk, eggs, and bread in it.

She showed us a Papa John's pizza store in front of our house and told us we could get dinner there. We loved pizza, so we went to Papa John's and picked up a large pizza for our first celebratory dinner in Canada. Although we were tired, the excitement and jet lag kept us from sleeping for a while.

CHAPTER 37

OUR FIRST DAY AND FIRST CHURCH EXPERIENCE

The doorbell woke us up to Barbara's arrival. She came to pick us up to help get our important documents done. The first few days were busy going from one government office to another for our health cards, etc. One day she showed us the library and our daughter's future school. I was overwhelmed by the school and the library. This was one of the most beautiful buildings I had seen so far. The thought of sending my daughter to school in this beautiful country filled me with thanksgiving.

Slowly, we learned how things were done in Canada. Within a few months, my husband found a job, and soon after our arrival, our daughter started her first school experience in kindergarten. We loved every moment of our new adventurous life.

On our first Sunday morning, we asked our host about the church nearby within walking distance. She knew we worked with the Anglican Church in Kampala, so she directed us to an Anglican church a few blocks away. We were excited about our first Canadian church service. We arrived at church and were greeted by an usher who gave us a bulletin. As we sat and the service began, we wondered where everyone was. Most of the pews were empty. Only a dozen people in their seventies attended the service. We didn't see anyone young. After the service, we stood for a while thinking someone would come and show us where to go now, but everyone left and went to the gym for coffee and a fellowship hour. We were the last ones to leave the sanctuary. As we were gathering our stuff to leave the church, the pastor approached and introduced himself, inviting us to the fellowship hour.

As we walked with him into the fellowship room, we took the coffee and cookies and sat at a table. Slowly sipping our drinks and munching on soft chocolate chip and oat cookies, we looked around, wondering why no one was talking to us. We were too new to figure out what was going on. After we finished our drinks, we left without talking to anyone. We couldn't figure out why no one greeted us and welcomed us that day. My husband and I walked quietly home, wondering about our first church experience.

CHAPTER 38

CANADIAN HOLIDAYS

After our first church experience at the Anglican Church, we didn't want to return. One evening, someone knocked at our door. We opened to see a black lady and a white lady standing there with bags in their hands. They told us they had come from a Gospel church and wanted to welcome us. We were overjoyed hearing they were from a Gospel church. We invited them in, and their gesture of love was amazing. They came to invite us to their Christmas banquet in December. After drinking tea and coffee together, they prayed with us and left. In the bags they left us were Christian books, new toys, a children's Bible, and some other things. We were deeply touched by their love and decided to go to their church the coming Sunday.

The next Sunday, we went to their church, and we truly felt welcomed. We saw people from all backgrounds. I still remember the message about Christian unity. After the service, the pastor announced the fellowship hour. My husband and I glanced at each other—we didn't want to go to the fellowship hour after our first experience. But the ladies who visited our home approached us after the service and took us to the fellowship room. They introduced us to everyone and asked us to tell them about ourselves—where we came from, who we were, etc.

Almost everyone came and talked to us after we told them about our lives in our birth country and our mission work in

Africa. A couple invited us to their Thanksgiving dinner then and there. We felt very much at home and decided we would attend.

It was October, the weather was getting colder, and leaves were falling off the trees. It was beautiful and magical. We often visited a big park a few miles away, and we were amazed at the changing colours of the leaves. We had never experienced this before.

Shops were decorated with pumpkins and haystacks. In all the stores, we saw these giant turkeys for sale. We had duck, alligator, and grasshoppers in Uganda, but turkey was something we had never tried. So, when our new friends hosted us for Thanksgiving dinner at their home, they filled us in about the traditions of Thanksgiving. They told us that in a few weeks, there would be a Santa Claus parade that we could watch from our bedroom windows, which we did. We loved our first few months in Canada and enjoyed every moment of them. Those were simple and happy days full of adventure, thanksgiving, and joy.

CHAPTER 39

CANADA EH!

A fter a few months living in Canada, we slowly began to realize how life could be so different and challenging here, how churches could be so cold and distant. In my first few years as a Christian, I had experienced Christianity in an African environment that was loud, joyful, and vibrant. Evangelism and telling others about Jesus Christ were at the core of every church and mission I worked with in Uganda, especially the Anglican Church of Uganda. When we started attending the Anglican Church in Canada, most of them had very little interest in reaching out. Most ministries and programs were designed to cater to the needs of the congregants. Most of them were very liberal and, to be honest, quite dry. We weren't sure what church to go to. There were so many different denominations to choose from. Most of them sounded biblical, but when we dug deeper, we found some heretical or seriously flawed views of Christology.

After a few years of attending several churches, I expressed my desire to a Baptist pastor to reach out to the world with the gospel message, but he didn't respond. Upon further inquiry, I was called into his office and given a long lecture about my role as a woman and why I couldn't talk about or teach the gospel. I was surprised to hear that. The pastor sounded like my Muslim father, who had similar views about women. I didn't know that there were several denominations in North America that still insisted that women remain quiet and not wear trousers or pants like men. I had no idea how badly the church in the West was divided over this issue of female pastors.

I was taught by my spiritual parents and my Ugandan father, Daddy Bishop, that every believer is called to share the gospel regardless of their race, colour, gender, or ethnicity. And here I was sitting in this beautiful office of this Baptist pastor, in one of the most advanced countries in the world, being told that as a woman, my role was to remain quiet and raise children at home. His second objection was that even though we had been attending for more than six months, we weren't official members. This revelation about how churches work in North America was new and honestly heartbreaking for us. We left the church and began to search for a different one.

It took us a few years to understand the denominational differences. Along the way, I learned that to become a pastor, most churches require a professional degree from an accredited seminary. I had always wanted to attend a Bible college, so obtaining theological education didn't bother me. I wanted to study the scripture deeply. But the denominational belief that women weren't allowed to preach bothered me for a long time until I asked my seminary professors.

After a few months of staying in our first home, we decided to move out west. We ended up in Calgary after briefly staying in Edmonton. We found good jobs in downtown Calgary. We lived and worked right in the downtown district a couple of blocks away from the train station. It was like we were living in a Hollywood movie set. We were situated among tall skyscrapers, beautiful downtown cafes, shops, and a light train in the middle. We loved the downtown life, and slowly, between full-time jobs and enjoying home life, my dream of attending Bible College faded away. We found a good church close to our home. It was a covenant church. We enjoyed the sermons and fellowship and started a Bible study at our home. We were enjoying our lives to the fullest, visiting the majestic and breath-taking Canadian Rockies every now and then. We didn't know that God would send us another test soon.

CHAPTER 40

ANOTHER TEST

Everything was going well. We had jobs, a nice apartment, an excellent school for our daughter, a car, and lived in a beautiful city. I found a good job with a big company that I was excited about, and we planned that once I finished probation, we could look for a house. But God had a different plan. I became pregnant with our second child. Everything went well with the pregnancy until my second-trimester ultrasound.

I was told that there was a serious issue and a chance that my baby might not survive. We were devastated and went to our knees. Once again, we were pleading for God to help us. No matter what the doctors and surgeons told us, we held onto the faith that we had experienced. I was sure that my baby would be fine, and I trusted God to heal her supernaturally as He had in the past.

But in my third trimester, the baby arrived prematurely, weighing only four pounds. I wasn't allowed to carry her. She was taken immediately to the ICU for operation in a few hours. I was certain that God wouldn't allow her to go through this surgery and would heal her, but when this happened, I was heartbroken. I didn't understand. Why didn't God hear any of my prayers? Why didn't Jesus heal her? My understanding of healing was superficial.

The next morning her surgeon told me that the surgery was a success. It wasn't what they expected, but our daughter had to stay in the hospital for a few more weeks. It was good news, but

I was still upset at God—why did he allow this suffering in my life while I had already suffered so much for Him? I was thinking like a Muslim, that I had sacrificed enough and done enough good works. After speaking with my pastor and being discipled by mature Christians, I understood why God sometimes doesn't allow healing and may sometimes permit suffering and trials.

Today, I look at my daughter and thank God for blessing her with a beautiful heart and amazing mind. She is one of the smartest children in her school, always acing everything she does. She is smart, loves the Lord, and has perfect health. She proudly shares her survival story with her friends at school and calls herself a miracle baby. What I thought was suffering and pain, God turned around for His glory, not only in her life but in our lives too.

As the days and weeks continued, God's faithfulness was always there. His blessings on my life continued and would continue to be experienced in the changes that would follow. After a few years in Alberta, we moved back to Ontario because I decided to attend one of the best Bible colleges in Canada.

CHAPTER 41

THEOLOGICAL EDUCATION

It was the best decision of my life. I had never been so satisfied and content. I loved every moment of every day I spent in the hallways of Tyndale University College and Seminary. My professors were hardworking and amazing Christians.

I grew in wisdom and knowledge of the Word of God. During my studies, my calling to preach the gospel was confirmed repeatedly. As a woman of colour coming from a conservative background and a former Muslim, it was a great privilege to be awarded a Master of Divinity degree. I was the only woman in my family to attend a post-secondary institution and be awarded a master's degree.

I had loved studying scripture ever since I discovered the Bible. So, I took full advantage of my freedom in Canada. I took courses in Biblical Hebrew and tried to understand scripture in its original language. I learnt about church history. I discovered during my studies that Christian history is preserved as it was. What I mean by that is, it is not censored. Everything good or bad done in the name of Christianity was openly taught and talked about. My professors weren't hesitant to talk about the shortcomings of the prophets in the Bible or cruel things done by so-called Christians in the name of religion. As a Muslim, I was taught that all prophets are sinless, and it was considered a great sin to associate sin with any holy man of Allah.

An observation from my studies is that Christianity teaches that all are sinners, including prophets, and only one is sinless— Jesus Christ, the Son of God. In contrast, Islamic history often overlooks the atrocities committed by most Muslim kings and leaders. I don't remember ever being taught in my Islamic studies class about any bad Muslim king. Every Islamic king was a good king, and because they were good, Allah gave them victory. While in my history of Christianity class, we were taught the good, the bad, and the worst of what the kings, queens, popes, and bishops had done. This transparency was rarely found in Islamic studies. I was growing in wisdom and knowledge, but the more I studied, the more I felt I didn't know. Even after holding a Master of Divinity degree in my hand, I still felt empty.

After I graduated from Tyndale, we moved out of the city. We thought it was time to buy our own house for our growing family. We moved to a smaller city.

After we settled, I started looking for a job. I was confident that with my Master of Divinity degree, many churches would be happy to hire me. But I was in for a bit of a surprise again.

I sent out hundreds of resumes over two years but rarely got a response from any church. I thought there was something wrong with my resume. So I started attending resume writing workshops. But the worker who checked my resume said everything looked good, actually very good.

I knew it would be hard for me as a woman of colour to find a job even in the egalitarian church, but I kept my faith and kept sending my resume. Some churches responded that I would be a good fit for "my ethnic group." Some said they preferred to hire a man of God, not a woman of God. I was getting a little upset, especially after more than two years of sending resumes. I was hurt at the worldly attitudes held by some of the pastoral search committees.

I specifically remember a church close to where I lived. I sent them my resume as I was willing to get credentials from their denomination. After weeks of waiting, I decided to follow up. They told me that they had already hired someone who had the right qualifications and experience. I thought maybe that wasn't meant for me.

Soon after, I started a church, and we needed to find a place to conduct services. I thought about that church and contacted the pastor there. To my surprise, I realized that the pastor was a very young man, had no previous experience in pastoring, and had no theological education except some courses from a Bible college and an undergraduate degree in a secular university. I was shocked when I heard this and wondered why the search committee had lied to me. It wasn't only sad but heartbreaking.

Meanwhile, I thought I should look for any kind of work to make ends meet. My bachelor's degree in commerce and accounting helped me find entry-level administrative work in an accounting firm, which didn't last very long. My supervisor had issues with me being a woman and an immigrant. On my last day of probation, I was told to quit or move to an hour away location. By that time, I had started a home church, and we were reaching out to non-Christians. Accepting their offer meant my ministry would have suffered, so I decided to quit.

It wasn't easy, but soon after that, God provided me with another job as an admin assistant in a large, Christian organization. At the time of writing, I am still working for this Christian organization. I love my work. I love the people I work with, and I love the way this Christian church and humanitarian organization is helping millions of people around the world while still holding onto the truths of the gospel.

My love of studying the Scripture drew me back to the Bible College. I was enrolled in McMaster Divinity College under their Master of Divinity program where I took Biblical Greek and some other courses. I was also accepted into their Doctor of Practical Theology program but due to my health, I had to defer the program. In the meantime, I am working on my Chaplaincy training certificate through Booth University. I was awarded a one hundred percent scholarship to attend this training program. It was totally unexpected and was not in my plan. God has a way of maneuvering my life in the direction He wants me to go, and I am glad that He is in charge.

He knows that the deepest desire of my heart is to be a Bible teacher in a Christian College but for now, I will stick to my chaplaincy training program fully paid by my work and I will serve the vulnerable and homeless population in my city. It is an honor and privilege to be used by God and to share His gospel with the world.

CONCLUSION

Currently, Christianity is under attack in almost every country, including countries supposedly considered Christian a few decades back and North America. In my twenty-four years of Christian life, I've never seen people hating Christians with the intensity that is happening right now. It only means that the Bible is the *only truth* in this world. Jesus warned His disciples in John 15:18 that the world would hate us because it hated Him first.

Everywhere I turn, I see the words of the Bible coming alive before my eyes. I am certain that Jesus is coming very soon, and I can't thank Him enough for saving me from the curse I was living under away from Him. It has been a long journey, a road marked with suffering but also with many joyous events.

I've had many disappointments, challenges, heartbreaks, hurts, and failures. There were times when I felt lonely, broken-hearted, and saddened by the way some Christian brothers and sisters treated me. But somehow, my Jesus appeared every time and gave me courage, bringing me someone to re-assure me that I'm on the right path.

My husband and I now pastor a church we started in our living room. We never thought we would make it this far, but we are in the seventh year of our ministry. We are a non-denominational church focused on reaching marginalized and sidelined individuals. Because we are non-denominational, we don't have a support system from a larger denomination. Churches in the region have come together to help with our ministry needs. We both work outside our church to support our family.

I am thankful to many partners and faithful people in our church who give from their limited resources to cover the rent and bills for the church building. On a minimum wage salary, paying for the cost of this book seemed like a giant challenge to me. I was putting off this project for many years due to the unavailability of the funds. Every time I tried to think about sending this book to the publisher, I had more pressing issues to deal with in my church or family.

Honestly, waiting is not my strong strength. But sometimes God wants us to wait for His timing and I am glad He made me wait despite my lack of patience. When I sent the manuscript to the publisher, I did not have a single dollar to my name. I did not know how I will pay for it, but God knew. He used people that I do not even know very well to pay for this project. I am deeply indebted to all my friends who financially supported this expensive venture. I especially would like to thank Dr. Susan Booth, Professor of Evangelism and Mission at Canadian Baptist Theological Seminary and College, in Cochrane, Alberta for her generous donation towards the cost of this book. Without her financial contribution, it would not have been possible to complete this project on time. I would also like to thank Dr. James Beverly Research Professor at Tyndale Seminary who encouraged me to send this book to the publisher. God truly is amazing and takes care of every detail. May this book become a reason for you to put your trust in our Lord Jesus Christ! Amen.

I have been asked if it is worth it to follow Jesus at the cost I paid. I cannot emphasize enough that following Jesus Christ was the best decision of my life. It is totally worth it to leave mother and father, sisters and brothers, family and friends, country, and culture to follow Jesus.

If God gives me a hundred lives, and in every life, He asks me to leave my family and follow Him, I pray that my answer would always be "Yes, I will follow you, Jesus."

I have tasted His goodness and His mercy. I know He is who He said He is. I know that "He will never leave me nor forsake me... He will be with me until the end."

Today, I invite you who are reading these words to follow Jesus. I can guarantee that it will be the best decision you will ever make. There will be trials and tribulations, there will be times when you will suffer, but in the midst of all this, He will hold you, He will be right beside you and comfort you. I pray that God will give you the courage to accept this invitation. Amen.

"For I am convinced that neither death nor life, neither angels nor demons, neither the present nor the future, nor any powers, neither height nor depth, nor anything else in all creation, will be able to separate us from the love of God that is in Christ Jesus our Lord." (Romans 8:38–39)